ATTEMPTS IN VERSE,

BY

JOHN JONES,

AN OLD SERVANT:

WITH

SOME ACCOUNT OF THE WRITER,

WRITTEN BY HIMSELF:

AND

AN INTRODUCTORY ESSAY

ON THE

LIVES AND WORKS OF OUR UNEDUCATED POETS,

BY

ROBERT SOUTHEY, ESQ.

POET LAUREATE.

LONDON:
JOHN MURRAY, ALBEMARLE STREET.
MDCCCXXXI.

LONDON:
PRINTED BY C. ROWORTH, BELL YARD,
TEMPLE BAR.

LIST OF SUBSCRIBERS.

A.

	COPIES.
The Lord Chief Baron Alexander	6
Miss Alexander, Airdrie House, Glasgow	6
Sir John D. Astley	1
The Rev. G. Alderson, Hornby, near Catterick	1
Captain Abraham, Royal Military College	1
Anonymous	12

B.

Duchess of Buckingham and Chandos	1
Hon. William Barrington	1
Rev. Henry Bishop, Holy Well, Oxfordshire	1
Mrs. Butler, Kingston, Lisle	1
Samuel Barber, Esq., Grasmere	1
G. C. Bedford, Esq.	4
Rev. Mr. Barham	1
Rev. E. Berens	1
— Bellases, Esq., 3, New Square	1
John Booth, Esq., Killerby, Catterick	1
N. Baily, Esq., Gallow Hill, Morpeth	1
Rev. J. Barnes, Rectory, Richmond, Yorkshire	1
Miss Bowe, Scorton, Catterick	1
Mrs. Boulton, Givon's Grove, Leatherhead	1
Miss Boulton, Epsom	2
Mrs. Barclay, Epsom	1
Dr. Bruce, Royal Military College	1
Lady Beaumont	1

LIST OF SUBSCRIBERS.

	COPIES.
William Sadlier Bruere, Esq.	6
Mrs. Sadlier Bruere	6
Miss L. Sadlier Bruere	1
Miss J. Sadlier Bruere	1
Miss Bagge, Stradsett, near Lynn	1
Miss Benn, Margaretta Farm, near Lynn	1
Hon. Sir F. Burton, Bart.	1
Lady Burton	1
Mr. Blackman, 9, Devonshire Place, Brighton	2
Mr. C. Brown, 13, New Bond Street	1
T. D. Belfield, Esq. Parson's Green	1
Mrs. Wade Browne	1

C.

The Marchioness of Cleveland, Raby Castle	2
Sir Foster Cunliffe, Bart.	1
Hon. Miss Courtney	1
J. Capel, Esq. M.P. 32, Russel Square	1
Mrs. Capel, ... Do.	1
Miss Capel, ... Do.	1
Rev. J. Cook, Kingston, Lisle	1
Miss Cooper, ... Do.	1
Rev. J. Cleaver, Cronwell	1
William Campbell, Esq., Portman Square	1
Thomas Charter, Esq., Lynchfield, Taunton	1
Miss E. Charter, Norton Fitzwarren, Taunton	1
J. T. Coleridge, Esq.	2
Mrs. Coore, Scruton Hall, near Bedale	1
Robert Colling, Esq., Haughton-Le-Skern, Darlington	1
Edward Carter, Esq., Theakstone Hall, Bedale	1
Major Coates, Priory, Andover	1
A. Campbell, Esq., Bedale	1
Mrs. Cary, Taunton	1
Mrs. Chaytor, Spenithorn Hall, Bedale	2

LIST OF SUBSCRIBERS.

COPIES.

Mrs. Costobadie, Wensley, near Leybourn	1
Mrs. Creswell, Lynn	1
Ralph Caldwell, Esq., Hilbrough near Swaffham	1
—— Cockerell, Esq., Westbourn Manor House, Paddington	1
Mrs. Cockerell .... Do.	1
Rev. W. Chester, Denton, near Harlestone	1

D.

The Bishop of Durham	5
Rev. Peter De Bary, 24, Newman Street	1
—— De La Chaumette, Esq. Bedford Place	1
Rev. Dr. D'Oyley, Lambeth	2
Mrs. D'Oyley, ... Do.	2
Mr. F. D'Oyley .... Do.	2

E.

Lady East	1
—— Earl, Esq., Ripon	1
Mrs. Edwards, Ashill, near Watton, Norfolk	1
James Everard, Esq., King Street, Lynn	1

F.

Sir William Foulkes, Bart., Hillingdon, Lynn	1
Lady Foulkes .... Do.	1
Richard Fuller, Esq., Holcomb, near Dorking, Surrey	1
Mrs. Fuller .... Do.	1
Joseph Fieldon, Esq., Witton House, Blackburn, Lancashire	1
Miss Fryer, Park Row, Leeds	1

G.

The Right Hon. Lady Harriot Gurney, Runeton, near Lynn	1
Lady Greenly, Titley, Herefordshire	1
Miss Gamon	1
Dr. Gooch, Librarian to his Majesty	6

	COPIES.
John Graves, Esq.	2
Rev. J. Griffiths, Emmanuel College, Cambridge	1
Rev. Wm. Glaister, Kirkby Fleetham, Catterick	1
Rev. Wm. Glaister, Jun., University College, Oxford	1
Henry Glaister, Esq., Bedale	1

H.

Sir Andrew Snape Hammond, Hammond Lodge, Lynn	1
Lady Hammond .... Do.	1
Rev. Dr. Hughes, St. Paul's	1
Mrs. Hughes ...... Do.	1
John Hughes, Esq.	1
Mrs. Hill, Streatham	2
Rev. J. B. Hunissen	1
Rev. Mr. Holmes	1
Rev. Mr. Halls	1
Rev. S. Hodson, Sharrow, Ripon	1
Mrs. Hodson ...... Do.	1
John Hodson, Esq., Brackamore, Ripon	1
John Holmes, Esq., Kennington	1
Mrs. Hastings, Titley, Herefordshire	1
Timothy Hutton, Esq., Clifton Castle, Masham	1
Mrs. Hutton .... Do.	1
Diaray Hutton, Esq., Aldborough Hall, Bedale	1
Thomas Hoseason, Esq., Banklands, Lynn	1
Mrs. Hoseason .... Do.	1
Miss Hoseason .... Do.	1
Mrs. Hawkes, Dereham, Norfolk	1
Thomas Hare, Esq., Stow Hall, near Downham	1
Hon. Mrs. Hood, 37, Nottingham Place	1

J.

George Jenner, Esq., Doctors' Commons	1
Mrs. Jarvis	1

K.

	COPIES.
Mrs. General Knight, 14, Portman Street	3
Rev. Mr. Knap, St. Paul's	1
Mrs. Kemplay, St. John's Place, Leeds	1
Mr. Kirby, Bedale	1

L.

Her Grace the Duchess of Leeds, Hornby Castle, Yorkshire	4
Lord Bishop of Llandaff	1
Lady Lethbridge	1
Miss Lethbridge	1
Mrs. Laurence, Studley Park	1
Rev. James Lynn, Keswick	1
Miss E. M. Lucas, 100, Gloster Place	1
J. C. Langlands, Esq., Bewick, Northumberland	1
Mrs. Langlands ...... Do.	1
O. Leefe, Esq., Richmond, Yorkshire	1
Rev. E. Lockwood, Bedford	1
Mrs. Lee Warner, Queber, Dereham, Norfolk	1

M.

Sir Alexander Malet, Bart., Gloucester Place	1
Lady Malet .... Do.	1
Mrs. Malet, Norton Fitzwarren, Taunton	1
Mrs. Maberly	1
John Monkhouse, Esq., Stowe, Herefordshire	1
John Melville, Esq., Harley Street	1
Rev. John Monson, Bedale	1
Miss Main, Richmond, Yorkshire	1
Mrs. Maltby, Bath	1
Mrs. Master, Croston Rectory, Chorley, Lancashire	1
Miss Penelope Master .. Do.	1

N.

	COPIES.
Rev. T. Newcome	1
Miss Newcome	1
Miss R. Newcome	1
Rev. Wm. Newsam, Scruton Rectory, Bedale	1
Miss Newsam .... Do.	1
Rev. James Newsam, Sharow, Ripon	1

O.

Rev. Wm. Otter, Stockwell Green	1
Mrs. Otter .... Do.	1
Mr. Wm. Otter .... Do.	1
Major Otter	1
Miss Otter, Bethel, near Morpeth	1
Rev. Edward Otter, Middleham, Yorkshire	1

P.

Honourable P. Pusey, Grosvenor Square	1
Honourable Lady Lucy Pusey .. Do.	1
Mrs. Peters, Glenalyn, Gresford	1
Henry Pattison, Esq.	1
Rev. Mr. Peckman	1
Colonel Pulleine, Crake Hall, Bedale	1
Mr. H. Pybus, Hook House, near Catterick	1
Captain Procter, Royal Military College, Bagshot	1
Dr. Pickering, .. Do.	1
Mrs. Parker, Ely	1
Mrs. Pepys, 48, Queen Anne Street	1

Q.

Edward Quillinan, Esq.	1

LIST OF SUBSCRIBERS.

R.

	COPIES.
Mrs. Geo. Rouse	1
Mrs. Redfern, Langton Hall, Darlington	1
Dr. Rumsey	1
James Robson, Esq., Crake Hall, Bedale	1
Henry Robinson, Esq., 5, Henrietta Street, Covent Garden	1
Mrs. Robinson .... Do.	1
Mr. Henry Raikes	1
Mrs. Rouviere, Yately, Hants	1
Rev. C. S. Ridley, University College, Oxford	1
Miss Roseboom, at Wm. Sadlier Bruere's, Esq.	1
George Rennie, Esq., 21, Whitehall Place	1
John Rennie, Esq. .... Do.	1
Mr. James Roberts, Leatherhead, Surrey	1
Mrs. Rickman	3

S.

	COPIES.
Mrs. James Stuart, Portland Place	1
Mrs. Smith, Thames Bank	1
H. Shrine, Esq.	1
Humphrey Senhouse, Esq., Nether Hall, Cumberland	1
Rev. Dr. Sleath	1
James Stephens, Esq.	2
Miss Storey, Bewick, Northumberland	1
Rev. John Swire Mansfield, Richmond, Yorkshire	1
Rev. Dr. Scot, Catterick	1
Miss Scot ...... Do.	1
Miss M. Scot .. Do.	1
Mr. Shepherd, Bedale	1
Miss Shuldham	1
T. Standart, Esq. Taunton	1
Mrs. Scroope, Danby Hall, Middleham	1
Dr. H. H. Southey, 1, Harley Street	1

T.

	COPIES.
The Countess of Tyrconnel, Kiplin, Catterick	1
The Rev. the Master of Trinity College	1
Henry Taylor, Esq.	1
Richard Twining, Esq.	1
George Twining, Esq.	1
J. A. Twining, Esq.	1
Rev. A. Townsend, Vicar of Northallerton	1
Rev. Chauncy Hare Townshend	1
Miss Emily Trevenen, Helston, Cornwall	1

V.

H. Villebois, Esq., Marham, near Swaffham	1

W.

The Right Hon. Charles Watkin Williams Wynn	1
The Lord Bishop of Winchester	1
William Wordsworth, Esq., Rydal Mount	1
Mrs. Whitbread	1
Mrs. Wood	1
Miss Wood	1
The Dean of Westminster	1
The Rev. Neville White	1
Jonathan Walker, Esq., Fencote, Bedale	1
Henry Witham, Esq., 78, Gower Street	1
Thomas Wright, Esq., Newcastle	1
Mrs. Wright .... Do.	1
Rev. James Wheeler, Clints, Richmond, Yorkshire	1
Rev. W. Wheeler, Royal Military College, Bagshot	1
Rev. J. Wells	1
Mr. Ward, 38, New Bond Street	1
Miss Worthington, Taunton	1
Miss Wingfield, 17, Bloomsbury Square	1
John Wiltshire, Shockerwick, near Bath	1
Rev. John Wood Warter, Christ Church, Oxford	1

CONTENTS.

	PAGE.
INTRODUCTION, WITH OBSERVATIONS ON UNEDUCATED POETS	1

ATTEMPTS IN VERSE BY JOHN JONES.

Some Account of the Author, written by Himself	171
The Author to his Book	181
The Journey of Life	183
The Snowball	185
Why that Sigh, &c.	196
Lines addressed to Mrs. Lawrence, Studley Park, Yorkshire	198
A Voice from Ripon	200
Deep in the Dell	202
An Address to a Dead Cat, which had fallen from the Ivy-tree that runs up the Tower of Kirkby Fleetham Church	204
Lines occasioned by walking over some Fallen Leaves	209
The Butterfly to his Love	212
To a wild Heath Flower	213
Old Mawley to his Ass	215
To the Tongue	220
To Lydia, with a Coloured Egg, on Easter Monday	226

CONTENTS.

	PAGE.
Hark! Hark! &c.	227
To Eliza, with a little Gold Key	229
The Friend of my Heart	230
Mary Killcrow	232
Home	238
An Address to a Violet	240
Jane Barnaby	243
Sally Roy	246
By Love we were led, Jane	247
A fanciful Description of a Passage down part of the River Wye, of a Cottage and its Inhabitants, &c.	249
Written in Alnwick Castle	262
The World's like a Tyrant, &c.	264
Laver's Banks	265
My Mary is no more	268
Reflections on visiting a Spring at different Seasons of the Year	270
Mary St. Clair	277
Orran and Bertha	278
The Children's Dirge at the Interment of a Gold Fish	283
An Excuse to a Young Lady for not writing some Verses on her Birth-Day	285
Written for a Young Lady to present to her Parents on the First Day of the Year 1825	286
Lines on parting from Miss H. when two years old	289
Thou tellest me, my Love	291
Louisa to Julia, with a Bunch of Flowers	293
To Maria, on her Birth-Day	294
To a Friend of Early Life, on her Birth-Day	296

CONTENTS.

	PAGE.
Lines written for Miss L. S. Bruere to present to her Mother on her Birth-Day	300
Lines addressed to the Misses L. and T. Sadlier Bruere, on the First Day of the Year 1824	301
Lines written for Miss L. S. B. to present to her Mother, on her Birth-Day, with some Primroses and Violets	303
Written for A. S. B. on his Birth-Day, when Eight Years old	304
On the Death of Lord Byron	306
On the Battle of Waterloo	308
Poor Kitty	311
Lines occasioned by reading a printed Bill in a Shop-Window at Richmond, Yorkshire	313
On the Death of Gaffer Gun	315
To a Gentleman who married a Second Wife in Three Days after the Interment of his First	317
My Nose	319
From a Cobler to B. on returning him an old Pair of Shoes	322
Verses written for a Boy to learn and repeat, who had committed a small Theft	324
A Prayer in Affliction	326
An Epitaph on Philip and Mary Jones	327
Lines on the Death of Miss Sadlier Bruere	328
To our worthy Shepherd, Mr. Way	331

INTRODUCTION.

LIVES AND WORKS OF OUR UNEDUCATED POETS.

INTRODUCTION.

BEING at Harrowgate with my family in the summer of 1827, I received there the following letter:

" SIR,

" THE person who takes the liberty of addressing you is a poor, humble, uneducated domestic, who, having attempted the stringing together a few pieces in verse, would be happy in the possession of your opinion of them.

" Living in a family, Sir, in which there are fourteen children, I have devoted but little time exclusively to their construction, they having been chiefly composed when in the exercise of my domestic duties, and frequently borne on my memory for two or three weeks before I had leisure to ease it of its burthen.

" Seeing in a Leeds paper, Sir, that you were at Harrowgate, I avail myself of the opportunity it affords me of soliciting the favour of your perusal of them, as well, Sir, from a conviction that I should be satisfied with your opinion, as that, from the kindness of your nature, you would forgive me if I intruded upon you what you could not in justice foster with your approval.

" Should it be your pleasure to inspect them, Sir, I shall be happy in sending them to you; and though it may not suit your present convenience, they might, in your possession, Sir, await a more favourable opportunity.

" The last of my humble attempts, Sir, occurred to me from seeing a lady of the family collecting the crumbs from the breakfast-table, and putting them by to await the coming of a little red-breast, who never failed to solicit them at the window during the winter months; and as it has just fallen from among some papers in which I placed it two or three months ago, not having room to insert it in my book, it suggested the idea of sending it as a specimen; and though, Sir, I can hardly hope that my poor little Robin possesses any trait of beauty worthy of your admiration, I do hope, Sir, that its harmless simplicity will obtain for me your pardon for the liberty I have taken in thus addressing you, and with that hope, Sir, I subscribe myself

" Your most respectful
and most dutiful servant,
JOHN JONES."

" AT W. S. BRUERE'S, ESQ.
KIRKBY HALL, NEAR CATTERICK,
Tuesday, 19th June."

THE RED-BREAST.

Sweet social bird with breast of red,
    How prone's my heart to favour thee!
Thy look oblique, thy prying head,
    Thy gentle affability;

Thy cheerful song in winter's cold,
    And, when no other lay is heard,
Thy visits paid to young and old,
    Where fear appals each other bird;

Thy friendly heart, thy nature mild,
    Thy meekness and docility,
Creep to the love of man and child,
    And win thine own felicity.

The gleanings of the sumptuous board,
    Conveyed by some indulgent fair,
Are in a nook of safety stored,
    And not dispensed till thou art there.

In stately hall and rustic dome,
   The gaily robed and homely poor
Will watch the hour when thou shalt come,
   And bid thee welcome to the door.

The Herdsman on the upland hill,
   The Ploughman in the hamlet near,
Are prone thy little paunch to fill,
   And pleased thy little psalm to hear.

The Woodman seated on a log
   His meal divides atween the three,
And now himself, and now his dog,
   And now he casts a crumb to thee.

For thee a feast the Schoolboy strews
   At noontide, when the form's forsook;
A worm to thee the Delver throws,
   And Angler when he baits his hook.

At tents where tawny Gipsies dwell,
   In woods where Hunters chase the hind,
And at the Hermit's lonely cell,
   Dost thou some crumbs of comfort find.

INTRODUCTION.

Nor are thy little wants forgot,
  In Beggar's hut or Crispin's stall;
The Miser only feeds thee not,
  Who suffers ne'er a crumb to fall.

The Youth who strays, with dark design,
  To make each well-stored nest a prey,
If dusky hues denote them thine,
  Will draw his pilfering hand away.

The Finch a spangled robe may wear,
  The Nightingale delightful sing,
The Lark ascend most high in air,
  The Swallow fly most swift on wing,

The Peacock's plumes in pride may swell,
  The Parrot prate eternally,
But yet no bird man loves so well,
  As thou with thy simplicity.

Sir Joseph Banks used pleasantly to complain that tortoise-shell tom-cats were the plague of his life, because every ignorant man or woman who happened to possess one, favoured him with the first offer of it, at fifty, or perhaps an hundred guineas below what, upon the faith of vulgar opinion, they believed to be the established price of so great a curiosity. For this flattering preference Sir Joseph was indebted to the high rank in the scientific world which he so deservedly held and filled so worthily: it was a tribute to his station and his character. Authors, and especially poets, who send their works for my perusal and opinion and advice thereon, have been as much the plague of my life as the tom-tortoise-shells were of his. Mr. George Coleman has no sinecure in his office of Licenser for the Stage; alas! the office which has thus been thrust upon me is a sine-salary, and the business itself is of a more ungracious kind. Two circumstances have drawn upon me this persecution; the publication of Henry Kirke White's Remains, and the appointment which I have the honour to hold of Poet Laureate,.. the Poet Laureate being supposed by many persons to be a sort of Lord Chancellor in Literature, a Lord Keeper of the King's taste, and to have the literary patronage of the public and the state at his disposal. The appointment itself has not exposed me to more sarcasms, as pungent as they have been new, concerning sack and sackbut, than this opinion has produced suitors to the High Court of Poetry over which I am supposed to preside. Know all men by these presents, that the Poet Laureate receiveth no allowance of sack; (the more's the pity!) and that any application to him in that, or any other capacity, for poetical preferment, from aspirant sons of song, might as well be addressed to the Man in the Moon.

Little likelihood then, certain readers will think, should there seem to have been, that Mr. John Jones would obtain such an answer to his application as he hoped for. But if there be some who think thus, many others I am sure there are whom it will not surprise to know, that the incipient displeasure which such a communication may be expected to excite, gave way as I perused his letter, and was completely dispelled by the verses: the former pleased me because of its simple humility; and in the latter, with all their imperfections, I saw something of Cunningham's vein, or of Cotton's, a man of higher powers, whom Cunningham followed. I read them to my wife and daughters, and to a lady of our party, whose approbation in the case of my own writings has long been to me an earnest of the only approbation which I am desirous to obtain, .. that of the wise, the gentle, and the good. They were pleased with the natural images and the natural feeling in these poor verses; and they were pleased, also, that instead of returning a discouraging reply and thus preventing any farther trouble to myself, I told my humble applicant he might send me his book, warning him, however, against indulging in any expectation that such poems would be found generally acceptable in these days;.. the time for them was gone by, and whether the public had grown wiser in these matters or not, it had certainly become less tolerant and less charitable.

Accordingly, the manuscript was sent me, and with it the letter which follows.

" KIRKBY HALL, NEAR CATTERICK,
23d June.

" SIR,

" I FEEL greatly obliged to you for your kindness in condescending to take the trouble of perusing my poor bits of verses. I am only fearful, Sir, that, even in your own expectations, you will not be gratified. Mine, Sir, have never been of a very sanguine nature. Had I been so fortunate as to come under your notice twenty years ago, your advice and encouragement might have made something better of me; but I am now, Sir, on the wrong side of fifty, and having never met with encouragement, and being generally very actively employed, I have not had leisure to seek for ideas, but only endeavoured to arrange those that came voluntarily, and that at times, Sir, when I have been too busily engaged to make a happy disposal of them. Consequently, Sir, my productions have been very limited, but from having had a little more leisure the last year, I have added several little pieces to my stock. Being on the Continent a few years, Sir, I attempted a long piece, which I intended denominating The Maid of the Wye, and under great difficulties I persevered in it for some time; but we were a large family in a small house, Sir, and from the repeated solicitations of some little favourites of the family, and from the noisy clamour of several Flemish maid-servants, and other causes, I became so disgusted with it that I gave it up, and could never again resume it. I have copied some passages of it into my book, the rest is destroyed; those you will find, Sir, entitled, A Fanciful Description of a Passage down the Wye; Fragments; and, I believe, all that run in the same metre, are parts of it. Should it be your opinion, Sir, that by weeding out a few of the worst pieces, and, if their faults were pointed out to me, correcting others, it would not be too contemptible to solicit a subscription for, I might as well, Sir, avail myself of any little benefit it might afford me; but if otherwise, Sir, I must beg of you not to let your kindness get the better of your judgement; for though I have had the bringing up of a family under circumstances which have subjected me to great difficulties, the struggle I trust is over, and if it has left me poor, Sir, my anxiety in respect to worldly prosperity is greatly diminished. It may be some gratification to your benevolent heart, Sir, to know that the interest you take in promoting the wishes of such an inferior being as myself, excites my gratitude; and when I tell you, Sir, that I have been upwards of twenty years in my present service, and that I possess the good wishes of every family it has been my lot to serve, I hope, Sir, it will impress you with a favourable opinion of my character. Believe me, Sir, I feel myself

Your much obliged and most dutiful Servant,

JOHN JONES."

This letter did not diminish the favourable opinion which I had formed of the writer from his first communication. Upon perusing the poems I wished they had been either better or worse. Had I consulted my own convenience, or been fearful of exposing myself to misrepresentation and censure, I should have told my humble applicant that although his verses contained abundant proof of a talent for poetry, which, if it had been cultivated, might have produced good fruit, they would not be deemed worthy of publication in these times. But on the other hand, there were in them such indications of a kind and happy disposition, so much observation of natural objects, such a relish of the innocent pleasures offered by nature to the eye, and ear, and heart, which are not closed against them, and so pleasing an example of the moral benefit derived from those pleasures, when they are received by a thankful and thoughtful mind, that I persuaded myself there were many persons who would partake, in perusing them, the same kind of gratification which I had felt. There were many, I thought, who would be pleased at seeing how much intellectual enjoyment had been attained in humble life, and in very unfavourable circumstances; and that this exercise of the mind, instead of rendering the individual discontented with his station, had conduced greatly to his happiness, and if it had not made him a good man, had contributed to keep him so. This pleasure should in itself, methought, be sufficient to content those subscribers who might kindly patronize a little volume of his verses. Moreover, I considered that as the Age of Reason had commenced, and we were advancing with quick step in the March of Intellect, Mr. Jones would in all likelihood be the last versifyer of his class; something might properly be said of his predecessors, the poets in low life, who with more or less good fortune had obtained notice in their day; and here would be matter for an introductory essay, not uninteresting in itself, and contributing something towards our literary history. And if I could thus render some little service to a man of more than ordinary worth, (for such upon the best testimony Mr. Jones appeared to be,) it would be something not to be repented of, even though I should fail in the hope (which failure, however, I did not apprehend) of affording some gratification to " gentle readers:" for readers there still are, who, having escaped the epidemic disease of criticism, are willing to be pleased, and grateful to those from whose writings they derive amusement or instruction.

It is evident that there could be no versifyers of this class in early times. The language of a Saxon thane was not more cultivated than that of the churl on his estate; indeed, the best as well as earliest of our Anglo-Saxon poets was in the lowest condition of freemen, and was employed as a night-herdsman when he composed his first verses. The distinction between the language of high and low life could not be broadly marked, till our language was fully formed, in the Elizabethan age: then the mother tongue of the lower classes ceased to be the language of composition; that of the peasantry was antiquated, that of the inferior citizens had become vulgar. It was not necessary that a poet should be learned in Greek and Latin, but it was that he should speak the language of polished society.

Another change also, in like manner widening the intellectual distinctions of society, had by that time taken place. In barbarous ages the lord had as little advantage over his vassal in refinement of mind as of diction. War was his only business; and war, even in the brightest days of chivalry, tended as surely to brutalize the feelings of the chiefs, and render their hearts callous, as the occupations of husbandry did to case-harden and coarsen the hind and the herdsman; but when arts and luxuries (of that allowable kind for which a less equivocal term is to be desired) had found their way from cloisters into courts and castles, an improvement as well of intellect as of manners, rapidly ensued. Then, also, the relations of states became more complicated, and courts in consequence more politic: the minds of the great grew at the same time more excursive and more reflecting; and in the relaxation which they sought in poetry, something more was required than the minstrels afforded in their lays, whether of ribaldry or romance. Learning being scarce, they who possessed a little were proud of exhibiting in their writings the extent of that small stock; and the patrons whom they courted, and who themselves were in the same stage of intellectual culture, were flattered at being addressed in a strain which must have been unintelligible to the multitude. When literature revived, the same kind of pleasure which had just before been given by a pedantic vocabulary, was produced by classical allusions, and imitations of ancient, or of Italian writers. The language then improved so suddenly, that it changed more in the course of one generation than it had done in the two preceding centuries; Elizabeth, who grew up while it was comparatively barbarous, lived to see it made capable of giving adequate expression to the loftiest conceptions of human imagination. Poets were then, perhaps, more abundant than they have been in any subsequent age until the present: and, as a necessary consequence of that abundance, all tricks of style were tried, and all fantasticalities of conceit abounded; they who were poets by imitative desire or endeavour, putting forth their strength in artificial and ambitious efforts, while the true poets held the true course,.. though the best of them did not always escape from what had thus been made the vice of their age.

The circumstances, therefore, of low breeding and defective education were so unfavourable, that the first person who, in a certain degree overcame them, obtained great notoriety, and no inconsiderable share of patronage. This was John Taylor, the Water-Poet, a man who has long been more known by name than by his writings. He was born in Gloucestershire, but at what place none of his biographers have stated in their scanty notices, nor has he himself mentioned in the volume entitled, " All the Works of John Taylor, the Water-Poet, being sixty-three in number, collected into one Volume by the Author, with sundry new Additions, corrected, revised, and newly imprinted, 1630." The book, though in height that of a modern quarto, would be catalogued among folios, for its shape; it is in fact neither, but of a nondescript size which may be called sexto, the sheet being folded into six leaves. It contains something more than 600 pages, in three series of paging, more than two-thirds consisting of verse closely printed and in double columns. Taylor lived twenty-four years after the publication of this volume, and published a great deal more; and though in this collection, (which is all that I have had opportunity of perusing,) there is some ribaldry and more rubbish, there is, nevertheless, so much which repays the search, that I wish the remainder of his works had been in like manner collected.

Young Taylor had an odd schoolmaster, upon whom some of his neighbours played a scurvy jest; the poor man was fond of new milk, and went to market for the purpose of buying a milch cow; but being short-sighted, and perhaps in other respects better qualified to deal with books than men, the seller, in sport it may be believed rather than roguery, sold him a bull, .. which poor "Master Green, being thus overseen," drove contentedly home, and did not discover the trick till he had called the maid to milk it. What happened to the pail in consequence called forth a memorial in four lines from his pupil, which was probably John's first attempt in verse. In other respects he was by his own account no very hopeful scholar: in that part of the poem called Taylor's Motto, which he entitles, " My "Serious Cares and Considerations," he says—

"I was well entered, forty winters since,
As far as *possum* in my accidence;
And reading but from *possum* to *posset*,
There I was mired and could no further get,
Which when I think upon with mind dejected,
I *care* to think how learning I neglected."

Having thus stuck fast in the thorns and brambles of the Latin grammar, he was taken from school and bound apprentice to a Thames waterman, perhaps as soon as he could handle an oar. The occupation is likely to have been his own choice, for it was well suited to his bold, hardy, and at that time, idle disposition; in those days, too, it was a thriving one, and gave employment to more men than any other trade or calling in the metropolis. Taylor, indeed, says, that "the number of watermen and those that lived and were maintained by them, and by the only labour of the oar and scull, betwixt the bridge of Windsor and Gravesend, could not be fewer than forty thousand." There may be some exaggeration in this; but when this assertion was made, the company was overstocked with hands, the circumstances which had occasioned its great growth and prosperity having changed. The first cause of its decline was the long peace which this country enjoyed under James I.: the Thames had been in time of war the great nursery for the navy; the watermen were "at continual demand" for the Queen's service, "as in duty bound," and good service they had done in all Elizabeth's wars. "Every summer 1500 or 2000 of them were employed" in her ships, "having but nine shillings and fourpence the month, apiece, for their pay; and yet they were able then to set themselves out like men, with shift of apparel, linen and woollen, and forbear charging of their prince for their pay, sometimes six months, nine months, twelve months, sometimes more; for then there were so few watermen, and the one half of them being at sea, those that staid at home had as much work as they would do." To their good fortune, also, for a while, the players at that time " began to play on the Bankside (Southwark) and to leave playing in London and Middlesex, for the most part." There were three companies playing there at once, " besides the bear-baiting;" and " then there went such great concourse of people by water, that the small number of watermen remaining at home were not able to carry them, by reason of the court, the terms, the players, and other employments; so that they were enforced and encouraged (hoping that this golden stirring world would have lasted ever) to take and entertain men and boys." Owing to this establishment of the three theatres on the Bankside, the company of watermen was increased more than half. But peace came, and the men who had been employed at sea returned to their old trade upon the river; and as misfortunes seldom come singly, (for a misfortune to the watermen peace was,) two of the three sets of players removed from the Surrey side to the Middlesex one, and there played " far remote from the Thames, so that every day in the week they drew unto them 3000 or 4000 people that were used to spend their monies by water." This reduced the watermen to great distress, and in 1613 they petitioned the King that the players might not be allowed to have a playhouse in London, nor within four miles of it, on that side the river; "the reasons that moved us unto it," says Taylor, "being charitably considered, make the suit seem not only reasonable, but past seeming most necessary to be sued for, and tolerable to be granted." He was selected by the company to deliver the petition and follow the business, which he did at the cost of seven pounds two shillings, for "horse-hire, horse-meat, and man's meat, expended in two journies to Theobalds, one to Newmarket, and two to Royston," before he could get the petition referred to the commissioners for suits. A counter-petition was presented by his Majesty's players, who said, that the watermen might just as reasonably propose to remove the Exchange, the walks in St. Paul's, or Moorfields, to the Bankside, for their own profit, as to confine them to it; "but our extremities and cause," says Taylor, "being judiciously pondered by the honourable and worshipful commissioners, Sir Francis Bacon very worthily said, that so far forth as the public weal was to be regarded before pastimes, or a serviceable, decaying multitude before a handful of particular men, or profit before pleasure, so far was our suit to be preferred before their's." A day was appointed for determining the business; but before it came, the chief commissioner, Sir Julius Cæsar, was made Master of the Rolls, by which means the commission was dissolved, and the case never came to a farther hearing. Had it proceeded, another proof would probably have been given, notwithstanding Bacon's opinion, that the convenience of the great public, when opposed to any part of that public, must ultimately prevail, even though the convenience gained should be trifling, and the injury sustained by the minor part of the most serious nature. Within our own memory, shoe-strings have prevailed over buckles in despite of ridicule, and covered buttons over metal ones in defiance of pains and penalties, in each case to the great detriment of what had been a flourishing branch of our manufactures. But the watermen were unreasonable in requiring that the Londoners, in that best age of the English drama, should, whenever they went to the play, be put to the discomfort and charged with the expense of crossing and recrossing the water; and that the players should be confined to the Bankside, where bad weather must so materially have affected their receipts.

Taylor complains in another of his pamphlets, that he and "many thousands more were much impoverished and hindered of their livings" by the proclamations which from time to time were issued, requiring the gentry to retire from the capital into their own countries. In certain despotic governments the sovereigns are said to have pursued the evil policy of keeping their nobles about the court, for the purpose of lessening their influence in the provinces, and rendering them dependent upon court favour and state employments, by involving them in habitual expenses beyond what their patrimonial revenues could support. No such erroneous views either of their own or the public interest were entertained by the kings of England; but this opposite policy, which required the landed proprietors to reside during the greater part of the year upon their own estates, seems, like the acts that were enforced against new buildings about London, to have originated in a prudent desire of keeping down both the size and population of the metropolis, because of the plague, visitations of which were then so frequent and so dreadful. This deprived the watermen of good part of their employ; and Taylor complains that his "poor trade," which had already suffered so much, was undone when hackney coaches came into use. The decay of what had once been a thriving occupation allowed him to engage in adventures which he might have been too wise to have undertaken if his fortune had been more prosperous.

But before this unfavourable change in his circumstances was felt, he had become known as the Water-Poet. His own account of the manner in which he took to the rhyming trade, may be understood to mean, that he was led to it by an imitative impulse, to his own surprise, and not very early in life.

" I that in quiet, in the days of yore,
 Did get my living at the healthful oar,
 And with content did live, and sweat, and row,
 Where, like the tide, my purse did ebb and flow;
 My fare was good, I thank my bounteous Fares,
 And pleasure made me careless of my *cares*.
 The watry element most plentiful,
 Supplied me daily with the oar and scull;
 And what the water yielded, I with mirth
 Did spend upon the element of earth.
 Until at length a strange poetic vein,
 As strange a way possest my working brain:
 It chanced one evening on a reedy bank,
 The Muses sat together in a rank,
 Whilst in my boat I did by water wander,
 Repeating lines of Hero and Leander.

>   The triple Three took great delight in that,
>   Call'd me ashore, and caused me sit and chat,
>   And in the end, when all our talk was done,
>   They gave to me a draught of Helicon,
>   Which proved to me a blessing and a curse,
>   To fill my pate with verse, and empt my purse."

These lines seem also to confess, that though he "left no calling for this idle trade," he had in some degree neglected one. It is, indeed, apparent, that he was a boon companion, neither unconscious of the wit and ready talents which he possessed, nor diffident of them; and though in his grammatical studies he had stuck at *posset*, he had been in a very good school for improving the sort of ability with which Nature had endowed him. Even as late as Dr. Johnson's days, a license of wit (if wit it may be called) was allowed to all persons upon the river, which would not have been tolerated any where else. Fluency in this sort of speech he could not choose but learn; and his vocation also brought him into conversation with persons of all descriptions, the best as well as the worst, especially when the theatres were on the Bankside. Moreover, he was not a mere fresh-water sailor; he had seen service enough to have entitled him to call himself an old seaman, if that denomination had in those days sounded more respectably than his own; for he had made no fewer that sixteen voyages in the Queen's ships, and was in the expeditions under Essex at Cadiz and the Azores. And no other occupation could have offered him such opportunities for reading as invited him in the intervals of chance leisure, even on his busiest days; in fact, he was a diligent reader; and although it was because of his low birth, low station, and want of regular education, that he obtained notice at first for his productions, there are many in these days who set up, not alone for simple authors in prose or rhyme, but as critics by profession, upon a much smaller stock of book-knowledge than Taylor the Water-Poet had laid in. Hear his account of his own studies!

> " I *care* to get good books, and I take heed
> And *care* what I do either write or read;
> Though some through ignorance, and some through spite,
> Have said that I can neither read nor write.
> But though my lines no scholarship proclaim,
> Yet I at learning have a kind of aim;
> And I have gathered much good observations,
> From many human and Divine translations.
> * * * *

The Poet* *Quid*, (or Ovid if you will,)
Being in English, much hath helpt my skill.
And Homer too, and Virgil I have seen,
And reading them I have much bettered been.
Godfrey of Bulloyne, well by Fairfax done;
Du Bartas, that much love hath rightly won;
Old Chaucer, Sidney, Spenser, Daniel, Nash,—
I dipt my finger where they used to wash.
As I have read these poets I have noted
Much good, which in my memory is quoted.

Of histories I have perused some store,
As no man of my function hath done more.
The Golden Legend I did overtoss,
And found the gold mixt with a deal of dross.
I have read Plutarch's Morals and his Lives,
And like a bee suckt honey from those hives.
Josephus of the Jews, Knowles of the Turks,
Marcus Aurelius, and Guevara's works;
Lloyd, Grimstone, Montaigne, and Suetonius,
Agrippa, whom some call Cornelius,
Grave Seneca and Cambden, Purchas, Speed,
Old monumental Fox and Holinshed;
And that sole Book of Books which God hath given,
The blest eternal Testaments of Heaven,
That I have read, and I with *care* confess,
Myself unworthy of such happiness."

The subject of his reading is one which he was

---

* Some jest is, I suppose, intended, which I cannot explain;—or, perhaps, it is pretended, to fill up the line.

evidently pleased with referring to, though he took care to ground his best claims for indulgence upon his " natural art." Wherefore, he says,—

>   ——— " do I take a scholar's part,
> That have no ground or axioms of art;
> That am in poesy an artless creature,
> That have no learning but the Book of Nature,
> No academical poetic strains,
> But homespun medley of my motley brains."

The first person who patronised him he addresses as " the Right Worshipful and my ever respected Mr. John Moray, Esquire:"—probably, the same " Mr. John Murray, of the bed-chamber to the king," whom Bacon calls his very good friend. Taylor has addressed this sonnet to him, and prefixed it to the earliest of his multifarious productions:

> " Of all the wonders this vile world includes,
>   I muse how flattery such high favours gain;
>   How adulation cunningly deludes
>   Both high and low, from sceptre to the swain.
>   But if that thou by flattery couldst obtain
>   More than the most that is possest by men,
>   Thou canst not tune thy tongue to falsehood's strain;
>   Yet with the best canst use both tongue and pen.
>   Thy sacred learning can both scan and ken

The hidden things of Nature and of Art.
'Tis thou hast raised me from Oblivion's den,
And made my muse from obscure sleep to start.
Unto thy wisdom's censure I commit
This first-born issue of my worthless wit."

This first-born had an odd name; he called it, in Tayloric style, " Taylor's Water-Work; or the Sculler's Travels from Tyber to Thames; with his boat laden with a Hotch-potch, or gallimaufrey of Sonnets, Satires, and Epigrams. With an ink-horn disputation betwixt a Lawyer and a Poet; and a quarterne of new catched Epigrams, caught the last fishing-tide; together with an addition of Pastoral Equivoques, or the Complaint of a Shepherd. Dedicated to neither Monarch nor Miser, Keaser nor Caitiff, Palatine nor Plebeian, but to great Mounsier Multitude, alias All, or Every One."

The manner in which he published his books, which were separately of little bulk, was to print them at his own cost, make presents of them, and then hope for " sweet remuneration" from the persons whom he had thus delighted to honour. This mode of publication was not regarded in those days so close akin to mendicity as it would now be deemed; pecuniary gifts of trifling amount being then given and accepted, where it would now be deemed an insult to offer and a disgrace to receive them. The method, however, did not always answer, and Taylor complains to this effect, though rather for others than for himself. He says,—

> " Yet to excuse the writers that now write,
> Because they bring no better things to light,
> 'Tis because Bounty from the world has fled;
> True Liberality is almost dead:
> Reward is lodged in dark oblivion deep,
> Bewitch'd, I think, into an endless sleep;
> That though a man in study take great pains,
> And empt his veins and pulverize his brains,
> To write a poem well, which being writ
> With all his judgement, reason, art, and wit,
> He at his own charge print, and pay for all,
> And give away most free and liberal,
> Two, three, or four, or five hundred books,
> For his reward he shall have—nods and looks;
> That all the profit a man's pains shall get,
> Will not suffice one meal to feed a cat.
> Yet noble Westminster, thou still art free,
> And for thy bounty I am bound to thee;
> For hadst not thou and thy inhabitants,
> From time to time, relieved and help'd my wants,
> I had long since bid poetry adieu;
> And therefore still my thanks shall be to you.

Next to the Court in general, I am bound
To you, for many friendships I have found.
There, when my purse hath often wanted bait
To fill or feed it, I have had receit."

Ben Jonson is one of the persons to whom he declares himself " much obliged for many undeserved courtesies received from him, and from others by his favour." And in a Dedication to Charles I. he says, ", My gracious Sovereign, your Majesty's poor undeserved servant, having formerly oftentimes presented to your Highness many such pamphlets, the best fruits of my lean and steril invention, always your princely affability and bounty did express and manifest your royal and generous disposition; and your gracious father, of everblessed and famous memory, did not only like and encourage, but also more than reward the barren gleanings of my poetical inventions." His Funeral Elegy, which he calls " A Living Sadness, duly consecrated to the Immortal Memory" of this " allbeloved sovereign Lord, the Peerless Paragon of Princes," concludes with these lines, addressed to all who read the poem.

" I boast not; but his Majesty that's dead
Was many times well pleased my lines to read,

And every line, word, syllable, and letter,
Were by his reading graced and made better;
And howsoever they were, good or ill,
His bounty showed he did accept them still.
He was so good and gracious unto me,
That I the vilest wretch on earth should be,
If for his sake I had not writ this verse,
My last poor duty to his royal hearse.
Two causes made me this sad poem write;
The first my humble duty did invite,
The last, to shun that vice which doth include
All other vices, foul ingratitude."

The Earl of Holdernesse was one of his good patrons, and moved King James to bestow a place upon him. What this place was does not appear in his writings, nor have his biographers stated: one office, which must have been much to his liking, he held at the Tower, by appointment of Sir William Wade; it was that of receiving for the lieutenant his perquisite of " two black leathern bottles or bombards of wine," (being in quantity six gallons,) from every ship that brought wine into the river Thames, a custom which had continued at that time more than 300 years. This was a prosperous part of Taylor's life, and if he did not write like Homer in those days, it was not for any failure in drinking like Agamemnon. He says—

> "Ten years almost the place I did retain,
>   And gleaned great Bacchus' blood from France
>   and Spain;
> Few ships my visitation did escape,
> That brought the sprightful liquor of the grape:
> My bottles and myself did oft agree,
> Full to the top, all merry came we three!
> Yet always 'twas my chance, in Bacchus' spite,
> To come into the Tower unfox'd, upright."

But the spirit of reform was abroad: the merchants complained that the bottles were made bigger than they used to be, and "waged law" with the lieutenant; and had it not been for the Wine-Poet's exertions, in finding and bringing into court those witnesses, who could swear to the size of the bottles for fifty years, they would have carried their cause. Poor Taylor was ill-rewarded for his services; no sooner had he established the right, than the office which he had held was put to sale, and he was discharged because he would not buy it. "I would not," he says, "or durst not, venture upon so unhonest a novelty, it being sold indeed at so high a rate, that whoso bought it must pay thrice the value of it."

"O bottles, bottles, bottles, bottles, bottles!
Plato's divine works, nor great Aristotle's,
Did ne'er make mention, that a gift so royal
Was ever bought and sold!"

He alludes to a loss of a different kind, in his "Navy of Ships and other vessels that have the art to sail by land as well as by sea," the names of these vessels being the Lord-ship, the Scholar-ship, the Lady-ship, the Goodfellow-ship, the Apprentice-ship, the Court-ship, the Friend-ship, the Fellow-ship, the Footman-ship, the Horseman-ship, the Surety-ship, the Wor-ship, and the Woodman-ship. In this tract there is some wholesome satire, and abundance of wit. The ship which he had been unlucky enough to embark in in this fleet, was the Surety-ship, of which he says, " she is so easy to be boarded, that a man need not trouble his feet to enter her, or use any boat to come to her,—only a dash with a pen, the writing of a man's name, passing his word, or setting his mark (though it be but the form of a pair of pot-hooks, a cross, a crooked billet, or a ⋀ for John Thompson,) any of these facile ways hath shipt a man into the Surety-ship during his life, and his heirs after him; and though the entrance into her be so easy, yet she is so full of impertinent and needy courtesy, that many men will lend a hand into her, with more fair intreaties, requests, and invitations, than are commonly used to a mask at the court, or a groce of gossips in the country; and being once entered, a tenpenny nail, driven to the head, may as soon scape out of an oaken post, as a man may get ashore again. She is painted on the outside with vows and promises; and within her are the stories of the tattered Prodigal, eating husks with the swine, the picture of Niobe, with Alecto, Tisiphone, and Megæra, dancing *lacrymæ*; her arms are a goose-quill or pen couchant, in a sheep-skin field sable; the motto above, *Noverint universi*; the supporters, an usurer and a scrivener; the crest, a woodcock; the mantles, red wax, with this other motto beneath, *sealed and delivered*. This ship hath the art to make parchment the dearest stuff in the world; for I have seen a piece little bigger than my two hands that hath cost a man a thousand pounds. I myself paid a hundred pounds once for a small rotten remnant of it. She is rigged most strangely; her ropes and cables are conditions and obligations; her anchors are leases forfeited; her lead and line are mortgages; her main-sails are interchangeable indentures; and her top-sails, bills and bonds; her small shot are arrests and actions; her great ordnance are extents, outlawries, and executions."

Taylor's productions would not have been so numerous if he had not gained something by them. If any celebrated person died, he was ready with an elegy, and this sort of tribute always obtained the acknowledgment in expectation of which it was offered. But it is evident, that he delighted in acquiring knowledge, and took pleasure in composition for its own sake, as in the exercise of a talent which he was proud to possess. His Memorial of all the English monarchs, from Brute to King Charles, was probably composed as much for this motive as to impress upon his own memory the leading facts of English history; then a set of miserable portraits cut in wood, without the shadow of resemblance till we come to bluff King Henry VIII., fitted it for popular and perhaps for profitable sale. It is, probably, from this bald and meagre chronicle in rhyme, which, for the subject, is likely to have been more common than any other of his tracts, that the commonly expressed opinion of his writings has been drawn, as if they were wholly worthless, and not above the pitch of a bellman's verses. But a more injurious opinion has seldom been formed; for Taylor had always words at will, and wit also when the subject admitted of its display. His account of the Books in the Old and New Testament, is in the same creeping strain. The best specimen of his historical verses is entitled God's Manifold Mercies in the Miraculous Deliverance of our Church of England, from the year 1565 until this present 1630, particularly and briefly described. This is in a series of what some late writers have conveniently called quatorzains,* to distinguish them from sonnets of proper structure: they are introduced thus:—

> "There was a Bull in Rome was long a breeding,
>   Which Bull proved little better than a Calf;
>   Was sent to England for some better feeding,
>   To fatten in his Holiness' behalf.
>   The virtues that this Beast of Babel had
>   In thundering manner was to bann and curse;
>   Rail at the Queen as it were raging mad;
>   Yet, God be thanked, she was ne'er the worse.
>   The goodly sire of it was impious Pius;
>   He taught it learnedly to curse and bann;
>   And to our faces boldly to defy us
>   It madly over England quickly ran.
>   But what success it had, read more and see,
>   The fruits of it here-underwritten be."

* It is remarkable, that Mr. Wordsworth should have cast his Ecclesiastical Sketches in a form so nearly similar. The coincidence (for I know Mr. Wordsworth had never seen Taylor's works, nor heard of this portion of them) may seem to show the peculiar fitness of this form for what may be called memorial poetry.

"This bull did excommunicate and curse the queen; it deposed her from her crown; it proclaimed her an heretic; it cursed all such as loved her; it threatened damnation to all subjects as durst obey her; and it promised the kingdom of heaven to those that would oppose and kill her."

He goes through the series of treasons which the bull produced, down to the Gunpowder-plot, and concludes with this Thanksgiving.

> " And last of all, with heart and hands erected,
> Thy Church doth magnify thy name, O Lord!
> Thy Providence preserved, thy Power protected
> Thy planted Vine, according to thy word.
> My God! what shall I render unto Thee,
> For all thy gifts bestowed on me always?
> Love and unfeigned thankfulness shall be
> Ascribed for thy mercies, all my days.
> To Thee, my Priest, my Prophet, and my King,
> My Love, my Counsellor and Comforter,
> To Thee alone, I only praises sing,
> For only Thou art my Deliverer.
> All honour, glory, power, and praise, therefore,
> Ascribed be to Thee for evermore."

These are no mean verses. Indeed, in every General Collection of the British Poets there are authors to be found, whose pretensions to a place there are much feebler than what might be advanced on behalf of Taylor the Water Poet. Sometimes he has imitated the strongly-marked manner of Josuah Silvester: sometimes, George Wither's pedestrian strain; in admiring imitation of which latter poet, (and not with any hostile or envious feeling, as has somewhere been erroneously stated,) he composed a piece which he called Taylor's Motto,—the Motto, (which is his only opposition to Wither) being, *Et habeo, et careo, et curo.* There is in Wither, when in his saner mind and better mood, a felicity of expression, a tenderness of feeling, and an elevation of mind, far above the Water Poet's pitch; nevertheless, Taylor's Motto is lively, curious, and characteristic, as well of the age as of the writer. It contains about fourteen hundred lines; and he tells us,

" This book was written (not that here I boast),
Put hours together, in three days at most;
And give me but my breakfast, I'll maintain
To write another ere I eat again;
But well, or ill, or howsoe'er it's penn'd,
Like it as you list; and so, I make an
END."

He has imitated Chaucer in a catalogue of birds, which though mostly a mere catalogue, has some sweet lines in it: and in other places he enumerates the names of rivers, the variety of diseases, and, more curiously and at greater length, the different trades and callings which were exercised in his days. Like poor Falconer, he made use also of his nautical vocabulary in verse.

" You brave *Neptunians*, you saltwater crew,
  Sea-ploughing mariners, I speak to you:
  From hemp you for yourselves and others gain
  Your spritsail, foresail, topsail, and your main,
  Top, and top-gallant, and your mizen abaft,
  Your coursers, bonnets, drablers, fore and aft,
  The sheets, tacks, bollens, traces, halliers, tyes,
  Shrouds, ratlings, lanyards, tackles, lifts, and gies,
  Your martlines, ropeyarns, gaskets, and your stays,
  These for your use, small *hemp-seed* up doth raise:
  The buoy-rope, boat-rope, quest-rope, cat-rope, port-rope,
  The bucket-rope, the boat-rope, long or short rope,
  The entering-rope, the top-rope, and the rest,
  Which you that are acquainted with know best:
  The lines to sound within what depth you slide,
  Cables and hausers, by which ships do ride:
  All these, and many more than I can name,
  From this small seed, good industry doth frame.
  Ships, barks, hoys, drumlers, craires, boats, all would sink,
  But for the ocum caulk'd in every chink.
  The unmatched loadstone, and best figured maps,
  Might show where foreign countries are (perhaps);

The compass (being rightly toucht) will show
The thirty-two points where the winds do blow;
Men with the *Jacob's* staff, and Astrolobe
May take the height and circuit of the globe:
And sundry art-like instruments look clear
In what horizon, or what hemisphere
Men sail in through the raging ruthless deep,
And to what coast, such and such course to keep;
Guessing by the Arctic or Antarctic star,
Climates and countries being ne'er so far.
But what can these things be of price or worth,
To know degrees, heights, depths, east, west, south,
    north.
What are all these but shadows and vain hopes,
If ships do either want their sails or ropes?
    And now ere I offend, I must confess
A little from my theme I will digress;
Striving in verse to show a lively form
Of an impetuous gust or deadly storm.
Where, uncontrolled, Hyperborean blasts
Tears all to tatters, tacklings, sails, and masts;
Where boisterous puffs of *Eurus'* breath did hiss,
And 'mongst our shrouds and cordage widely whiz;
Where thundering *Jove*, amidst his lightning flashing,
Seem'd overwhelmed with *Neptune's* mountain dashing;
Where glorious *Titan* hid his burning light,
Turning his bright meridian to black night;
Where blustering *Eole* blew confounding breath,
And thunder's fearfull larum threatened death;

Where skies and seas, hail, wind, and slavering sleet,
As if they all at once had meant to meet
In fatal opposition, to expire
The world, and unto *Chaos* back retire.
Thus, while the Winds' and Sea's contending gods,
In rough robustious fury are at odds,
The beaten ship, tost like a forceless feather,
Now up, now down, and no man knowing whither:
The topmast some time tilting at the moon,
And being up doth fall again as soon,
With such precipitating low descent,
As if to hell's black kingdom down she went.
Poor ship that rudder on no steerage feels,
Sober, yet worse than any drunkard reels,
Unmanaged, guideless, too and fro she wallows,
Which (seemingly) the angry billows swallows.

A Storm.

'Midst darkness, lightning, thunder, sleet, and rain,
Remorseless winds and mercy-wanting main,
Amazement, horror, dread from each man's face
Had chased away life's blood, and in the place
Was sad despair, with hair heaved up upright,
With ashy visage, and with sad affright,
As if grim death with his all-murdering dart,
Had aiming been at each man's bloodless heart.
Out cries the master, ' Lower the topsail, lower !'
Then up aloft runs scrambling three or four,
But yet for all their hurly burly hast,
Ere they got up, down tumbles sail and mast.

'Veer the main-sheet there,' then the master cried,
'Let rise the fore-tack, on the larboard side:
Take in the fore-sail, yare, good fellows, yare,
Aluffe at helm there,—ware, no more, beware,
Steer south-south-east there, I say ware no more,
We are in danger of the leeward shore,
Clear your main-brace, let go the bolein there,
Port, port the helm hard, Romer, come no near.
Sound, sound, heave, heave the lead, what depth,
    what depth?'
'Fathom and a half, three all.'
Then with a whiff, the winds again do puff,
And then the master cries 'Aluff, aluff,
Make ready the anchor, ready the anchor, hoa,
Clear, clear the boigh-rope, steddy, well steer'd so;
Hale up the boat; in sprit-sail there afore,
Blow wind and burst, and then thou wilt give o'er.
Aluff, clap helm a-lee, yea, yea, done, done,
Down, down alow, into the hold quick run.
There's a plank sprung, something in hold did break,
Pump—bullies,—carpenters, quick stop the leak.
Once heave the lead again, and sound abaffe.'
'A shafnet less, seven all.'
'Let fall the anchor then, let fall,
Man, man the boat, a woat hale, up hale,
Top your main yard a port, veer cable alow,
Go way a-head the boat there hoe, dee row,
Well pumpt, my hearts of gold, who says amends,
East and by south, west and by north she wends,

This was a weather with a witness here,
But now we see the skies begin to clear,
To dinner, hey, and let's at anchor ride,
Till wind grows gentler, and a smoother tide.'

"*I think*," he pursues in prose, "*I have spoken Heathen Greek, Utopian, or Bermudian, to a great many of my readers in the description of this storm, but indeed I wrote it only for the understanding mariner's reading. I did it three years since, and could not find a better place than this to insert it, or else it must have lain in silence.*"

In this prose postcript Taylor alludes to some epitaphs in gibberish upon Tom Coryat the Odcombian, whose harmless eccentricities made him the butt of all wits and witlings, his contemporaries. Sometimes he amused himself with verses of grandiloquous nonsense,—not that kind of nonsense which passes for sense and sublimity with the poet himself, and is introduced as such to the admiration of the world by some literary master of the ceremonies;—but honest right rampant nonsense.

"Think'st thou a wolf thrust through a sheepskin
    glove,
Can make me take this goblin for a lamb?
Or that a crocodile in barley-broth
Is not a dish to feast Don Belzebub?

> Give me a medlar in a field of blue
> Wrapt up stigmatically in a dream,
> And I will send him to the gates of Dis,
> To cause him fetch a sword of massy chalk
> With which he won the fatal Theban field
> From Rome's great mitred metropolitan."

Among his exhibitions of metre are some sonnets, as he calls them, composed upon one rhyme: one little piece in which all the lines rhyme upon *Coriat,* and another in which *crudities* is the key-word,—levelled against the same poor inoffensive humourist, who, ridiculous as he was, and liked to make himself, is nevertheless entitled to some respect for his enterprising spirit, his perseverance, and his acquirements; and to some compassion for his fate. It may be more worthy of notice, that Hudibrastic rhymes are to be found in the Water-Poet's works: there may be earlier specimens, and probably are, for Taylor possessed an imitative rather than inventive talent; but this is the earliest that I have seen.

Whether from this itch of imitation, or the love of adventure, or want of other employment, and the desire of gain, Taylor engaged at different times in expeditions which were characterised by some singularity, or some difficulty, and even danger. Such undertakings were not uncommon at that time. His "loving friend," Samuel Rowlands, in some verses addressed to him upon his, "Sculler's Travels from Tiber to Thames," enumerates some of those which had attracted most notice.

> "Ferris gave cause of vulgar wonderment,
> When unto Bristow* in a boat he went:
> Another with his sculler ventured more,
> That rowed to Flushing from our English shore:
> Another did devise a wooden whale
> Which unto Calais did from Dover sail:
> Another with his oars and slender wherry
> From London unto Antwerp o'er did ferry:
> Another, maugre fickle fortune's teeth,
> Rowed hence to Scotland and arrived at Leith."

These were all wagering adventures. The first which Taylor undertook (in the year 1616) he published an account of, with this title, "Taylor's Travels, three weeks, three days, and three hours' observations, from London to Hamburg, in Germany, amongst Jews and Gentiles; with descriptions of Towns and Towers, Castles and Citadels, artificial Gallowses and natural Hangmen, dedicated for the present to the absent Odcombian

---

* A tract describing this adventure, and the honours with which the adventurers were entertained at Bristol, is noted in that very valuable repository of literary information, the British Bibliographer, vol. ii.

knight errant, Sir Thomas Coriat, Great Britain's Error, and the world's Mirror." He had a brother settled in a town which he calls Buckaburgh, in the earldom of Schomberg; and the motive for this journey was to visit him: but he thought it might be turned to some account also, by finding persons who would receive money from him, and pay him back a larger sum if he performed the specified journey, and returned from it. I have to thank him for the story of Roprecht the Robber, which I found in his account of this journey. It seems that he made a second to the same country, but there is only a bare intimation of this in the collected volume of his works. His third undertaking was to travel on foot from London to Edinburgh, " not carrying any money to or fro; neither begging, borrowing, or asking meat, drink, or lodging." This he performed in 1618, and published an account of it in verse and prose, entitled " The Pennyless Pilgrimage, or the Moneyless Perambulation of John Taylor, alias the King's Majesty's Water-Poet." " This journey," says he, " was undertaken, neither in imitation or emulation of any man, but only devised by myself, on purpose to make trial of my friends, both in this kingdom of England and that of Scotland, and because I would be an eye-witness of divers things which I had heard of that country. And whereas many shallow-brained critics do lay an aspersion on me that I was set on by others, or that I did undergo this project either in malice or mockery of Master Benjamin Jonson, I vow, by the faith of a Christian, that their imaginations are all wild; for he is a gentleman to whom I am so much obliged, for many undeserved courtesies that I have received from him, and from others by his favour, that I durst never to be so impudent or ingrateful, as either to suffer any man's persuasions, or mine own instigation, to make me to make so bad a requital for so much goodness."

The undertaking was no very arduous one, for he was at that time a well-known person: he counted (as appears by his own words) on his friends upon the road; he carried, in his tongue, a gift which, wherever he might be entertained, would be accepted as current payment for his entertainment; and moreover, he had his man to accompany him, and a sumpter-beast well victualled for the journey.

" There in my knapsack to pay hunger's fees,
  I had good bacon, bisket, neat's tongue, cheese,

> With roses, barberries, of each conserves,
> And mithridate that vigorous health preserves;
> And, I intreat you take these words for no lies,
> I had good aquavita, rosasolies,
> With sweet ambrosia, the gods' own drink,
> Most excellent gear for mortals, as I think;
> Besides I had both vinegar and oil."

Thus provided he set forth, baiting and lodging as he went with friend or acquaintance, or at the cost or invitation of good-natured strangers. He says—

"I made my legs my oars, and rowed by land."

But he, and probably his man too, had been more used to ply their arms than their legs, for they were poor pedestrians; and had nearly foundered by the time they reached Daventry. It had been a wet and windy day, and meeting with something like Tom Drum's entertainment from the hostess of the Horse-shoe in that town, who had "a great wart rampant on her snout," they were fain

> ———————— " to hobble seven miles more,
> The way to Dunchurch, foul with dirt and mire,
> Able, I think, both man and horse to tire:
> On Dunsmore-heath, a hedge doth then enclose
> Grounds on the right-hand, there I did repose.

Wit's whetstone, Want, then made us quickly learn,
With knives to cut down rushes and green fern,
Of which we made a field-bed in the field,
Which sleep and rest and much content did yield.
There with my mother Earth I thought it fit
To lodge.—
My bed was curtained with good wholesome airs,
And being weary, I went up no stairs;
The sky my canopy; bright Phœbe shin'd;
Sweet bawling Zephyrus breath'd gentle wind;
In heaven's star-chamber I did lodge that night,
Ten thousand stars me to my bed did light.
There barricadoed with a bank lay we,
Below the lofty branches of a tree.
There my bedfellows and companions were,
My man, my horse, a bull, four cows, two steer;
But yet for all this most confused rout,
We had no bed-staves, yet we fell not out.
Thus Nature, like an ancient free upholster,
Did furnish us with bedstead, bed, and bolster;
And the kind skies (for which high Heaven be
    thanked!)
Allowed us a large covering, and a blanket."

Proceeding the next day " through plashes, puddles, thick, thin, wet, and dry," he reached Coventry, and was there entertained two or three days by Dr. Holland, the once well-known Philemon, who used, in translation, more paper and fewer pens than any other writer before or since; and who " would not let Suetonius be Tranquillus." After leaving him, he was welcomed at Lichfield by an acquaintance, who offered him money also, which it was against the bond to accept, and supplied him with " good provant." The next day's was no pleasant journey.

" That Wednesday I a weary way did pass,
  Rain, wind, stones, dirt, and dabbling dewy grass,
  With here and there a pelting scattered village,
  Which yielded me no charity or pillage;
  For all the day, nor yet the night that follow'd,
  One drop of drink I am sure my gullet swallow'd.
  At night I came to a stony town call'd Stone,
  Where I knew none, nor was I known of none.
  I therefore through the streets held on my pace,
  Some two miles farther, to some resting place.
  At last I spied a meadow newly mowed,
  The hay was rotten, the ground half o'er-flowed:
  We made a breach and entered, horse and man,
  There our pavilion we to pitch began,
  Which we erected with green broom and hay,
  To expel the cold and keep the rain away;
  The sky all muffled in a cloud 'gan lower,
  And presently there fell a mighty shower,
  Which without intermission down did pour
  From ten at night until the morning's four.
  We all this time close in our couch did lie,
  Which being well compacted kept us dry."

Sir Urien Legh entertained him with right old hospitality at Adlington, near Macclesfield, from the Thursday-night till Monday-noon,—having him at his own table; though Taylor had not "shifted a shirt" since he left London. Sir Urien gave him a letter to his kinsman, Edmund Prestwitch, a good esquire, near Manchester; there he was lodged and fed, and shaved, and his horse (for the second time) shod; and for this gentleman's sake he was sumptuously entertained by the people of Manchester, Mr. Prestwitch sending a man and horse to guide him, and bear his expenses through the county. But his recommendation sufficed in lieu of all charges at Manchester: the kindness which he there experienced, Taylor thus relates:—

"Their loves they on the tenter-hooks did rack,
  Roast, boiled, baked, too-too-much, white, claret, sack;
Nothing they thought too heavy, or too hot,
Cann followed cann, and pot succeeded pot.
Thus what they could do, all they thought too little,
Striving in love the traveller to whittle.
We went into the house of one John Pinners,
(A man that lives amongst a crew of sinners,)
And there eight several sorts of ale we had,
All able to make one stark drunk, or mad.

"But I with courage bravely flinched not,
And gave the town leave to discharge the shot.
We had at one time set upon the table,
Good ale of Hyssop (twas no Esop-fable):
Then had we ale of Sage, and ale of Malt,
And ale of Wormwood that could make one halt;
With ale of Rosemary, and of Bettony,
And two ales more, or else I needs must lie.
But to conclude this drinking aley tale,
We had a sort of ale called Scurvy ale.
Thus all these men at their own charge and cost
Did strive whose love should be expressed most;
And farther to declare their boundless loves,
They saw I wanted, and they gave me, gloves."

The hostess, also, of the Eagle and Child, had his shirts and bands washed, and gave him twelve silk points. The same recommendation procured him a good reception at Preston, where he tarried three days, and protests that he never saw a town more wisely governed by the law. "Kind Master Thomas Banister," the mayor, spent much cost and charge upon him, and rode with him at his departure two miles on his way.

"There by good chance I did more friendship get,
The under-shriefe of Lancashire we met,
A gentleman that loved and knew me well,
And one whose bounteous mind doth bear the bell.

There, as if I had been a noted thief,
The Mayor delivered me unto the Shriefe;
The Shriefe's authority did much prevail,
He sent me unto one that kept the jail.
Thus I, perambulating poor John Taylor,
Was given from Mayor to Shriefe, from Shriefe to Jailor.
The Jailor kept an inn, good beds, good cheer,
Where, paying nothing, I found nothing dear,
For the under-shriefe, kind Master Covill named,
(A man for house-keeping renowned and famed,)
Did cause the town of Lancaster afford
Me welcome, as if I had been a lord."

Master Covill sent a man with him to Sedbergh, which was two days' journey, and they scarcely missed an alehouse on the way, so liberal was the guide of his master's money. The next stage was to Master Edmund Branthwaite's, at Carling Hill. Branthwaite escorted him to Orton, where Master Corney, "a good true divine," was his host; and Master Corney sent a man with him "o'er dale and down, who lodged and boarded him at Peereth (Penrith) town." There he found a volunteer guide for Carlisle; but two miles wide of that city Sir John Dalstone entertained him. One might have hoped in these parts for a happy meeting between John Taylor and Barnabee, of immortal memory;

indeed, it is likely that the Water-Poet and the Anti-Water-Poet were acquainted, and that the latter may have introduced him to his connections hereabout, Branthwaite being the same name as Brathwait, and Barnabee's brother having married a daughter of this Sir John Dalstone. He makes his acknowledgments also to Sir Henry Curwen, for good offices at Carlisle. Adam Robinson, who had been mayor of that city the preceding year, provided him with a guide to Edinburgh, which, of the many helps upon his journey, was the greatest. Having crost the border, he then proceeds with his narrative in prose.

He waded the Esk and the Annan, and reached Moffatt in one day from Carlisle—" the weariest day's journey that ever he footed." The next day brought him one-and-twenty miles to a sorry village called Blithe; " but I was blithe myself," he says, " to come to any place of harbour or succour; for since I was born I never was so weary, or so near being dead with extreme travel. I was foundered and refoundered of all four; and for my better comfort, I came so late, that I must lodge without doors all night, or else in a farmhouse where the good wife lay in child-bed, her husband being from home, her own servant maid being her nurse; a creature naturally compacted and artificially adorned with an incomparable homeliness." Hence it was but fifteen miles to Edinburgh, in which " wished, long-expected, ancient, famous city," he came to take rest on the 13th of August, having started from London on the 14th of July.

." I entered like Pierce Pennyless, altogether moneyless, but, I thank God, not friendless; for, being there, for the time of my stay, I might borrow—if any man would lend; spend—if I could get; beg—if I had the impudence; and steal—if I durst adventure the price of a hanging. But my purpose was to house my horse, and to suffer him and my apparel to lie in durance, or lavender, instead of litter, till such time as I could meet with some valiant friend that would desperately disburse. Walking thus down the street, (my body being tired with travel, and my mind attired with moody, muddy, Moor-ditch melancholy,) my contemplation did devoutly pray, that I might meet one or other to prey upon, being willing to take any slender acquaintance of any map whatsoever; viewing and circumviewing every man's face I met, as if I meant to draw his picture; but all my acquaintance was *non est inventus:* (pardon me, reader, that Latin is none of my own, I swear by Priscian's pericranium, an oath which I have ignorantly broken many times!) At last I resolved that the next gentleman that I met withal, should be acquaintance whether he would or no: and presently fixing mine eyes upon a gentleman-like object, I looked on him as if I would survey something through him, and make him my perspective. And he much musing at my gazing, and I much gazing at his musing, at last he crossed the way and made toward me, and then I made down the street from him, leaving him to encounter with my man, who came after me, leading my horse; whom he thus accosted: 'My friend,' quoth he, 'doth yonder gentleman' (meaning me) 'know me, that he looks so wistly on me?' 'Truly Sir,' said my man, 'I think not: but my master is a stranger come from London, and would gladly meet some acquaintance to direct him where he may have lodging, and horse-meat.' Presently the gentleman (being of a generous disposition) overtook me, with unexpected and undeserved courtesy, brought me to a lodging, and caused my horse to be put into his own stable: whilst we, discoursing over a pint of Spanish, I related so much English to him, as made him lend me ten shillings: (his name was Master John Maxwell,) which money, I am sure, was the first that I handled after I came from out the walls of London."

The gentleman who with so much good-nature allowed this acquaintanceship to be thus forced on him, walked about the city with him. Taylor had seen many fortresses in Germany, the Netherlands, Spain, and England, but all, he thought, must give place to Edinburgh Castle, both for strength and situation, and the High Street was " the fairest and goodliest" that ever his eyes beheld, as well as the largest that he had ever heard of; " the buildings being all of squared stone, five, six, and seven stories high, and many bye-lanes and closes on each side of the way, wherein are gentlemen's houses, much fairer than the buildings in the High Street; for in the High Street the merchants and tradesmen do dwell; but the gentlemen's mansions and goodliest houses are obscurely founded in the aforesaid lanes; the walls are eight or ten feet thick, exceeding strong, not built for a day, a week, or a month, or a year, but from antiquity to posterity, for many ages." Here he soon found, or made, so many acquaintances, and those so liberal of their wine and ale, that he says, if any man had asked him a civil question every night before he went to bed, all the wit in his head could not have made him a sober answer.

At length he met with Master Bernard Lindsay, one of the grooms of his Majesty's bedchamber: " he knew my estate was not guilty, because I brought no guilt with me, more than my sins, (and they would not pass current there): he therefore did replenish the vastity of my empty purse, and discharged a piece at me with two bullets of gold, each being in value worth eleven shillings, white money." He was now in the way of old court acquaintance, and here he gives us an anecdote of his life which well illustrates the utility and capacity of the article of dress known in those days by the appellation of trunk-hose.

" I went two miles from Leith, to a town called Burnt-Island, where I found many of my especial good friends, as Master Robert Hay, one of the grooms of his Majesty's bedchamber; Master David Drummond, one of his gentlemen-pensioners; Master James Acmooty, one of the grooms of the privy-chamber; Captain Murray; Sir Henry Witherington, knight; Captain Tyrie, and divers others: and there Master Hay, Master Drummond, and the good old Captain Murray, did very bountifully furnish me with gold for my expenses; but

I being at dinner with these aforesaid gentlemen, as we were discoursing, there befell a strange accident, which I think worth the relating.

"I know not upon what occasion they began to talk of being at sea in former times, and I (amongst the rest) said, I was at the taking of Cales: whereto an English gentleman replied, that he was the next good voyage after at the Islands. I answered him that I was there also. He demanded in what ship I was? I told him in the Rainbow of the Queen's: why (quoth he) do you not know me? I was in the same ship, and my name is Witherington. Sir, said I, I do remember the name well; but by reason that it is near two-and-twenty years since I saw you, I may well forget the knowledge of you. Well, said he, if you were in that ship, I pray you tell me some remarkable token that happened in the voyage; whereupon I told him two or three tokens, which he did know to be true. Nay, then, said I, I will tell you another, which (perhaps) you have not forgotten. As our ship and the rest of the fleet did ride at anchor at the Isle of Flores, (one of the isles of the Azores,) there were some fourteen men and boys of our ship that for novelty would go ashore, and see what fruit the island did bear, and what entertainment it would yield us: so being landed, we went up and down and could find nothing but stones, heath, and moss, and we expected oranges, lemons, figs, musk-millions, and potatoes: in the mean space the wind did blow so stiff, and the sea was so extreme rough, that our ship-boat could not come to the land to fetch us, for fear she should be beaten in pieces against the rocks; this continued five days, so that we were almost famished for want of food; but at the last, (I, squandering up and down,) by the providence of God, I happened into a cave or poor habitation, where I found fifteen loaves of bread, each of the quantity of a penny loaf in England; I, having a valiant stomach of the age of almost a hundred and twenty hours breeding, fell to, and ate two loaves and never said grace; and as I was about to make a horse-loaf of the third loaf, I did put twelve of them into my breeches, and my sleeves, and so went mumbling out of the cave, leaning my back against a tree, when upon the sudden a gentleman came to me, and said, friend, what are you eating? Bread (quoth I). For God's sake, said he, give me some! With that I put my hand into my breech, (being my best pantry,) and I gave him a loaf, which he received with many thanks, and said that if ever he could requite it he would. I had no sooner told this tale, but Sir Henry Witherington did acknowledge himself to be the man that I had given the loaf unto two-and-twenty years before; where I found the proverb true, that men have more priviledge than mountains in meeting."

Taylor now departed from Edinburgh, meaning to see Stirling Castle, visit his " honourable friends" the Earl of Marr and Sir William Murray, Lord of Abercarney, and return in two days. But when he came to Stirling he found that these friends were gone to the great hunting in the Brea of Marr, and he was told, that if he made haste, he might perhaps overtake them at Brechin. When he reached Brechin, they had been gone four days. So taking another guide, after them he went, by " strange ways, over mountains and rocks, putting up the first night in the Laird of Eggel's land, at a house where the people could scarcely speak any English," and where, for the only time in Scotland, he was annoyed by the most unclean of six-legged insects, which he calls Irish musquitoes. Next day he travelled over Mount Skeene; it was warm in the valley, " but when I came to the top," he says, " my teeth began to dance in my head with cold, like virginals' jacks, and withal, a most familiar mist embraced me round, that I could not see through my length any way; withal, it yielded so friendly a dew, that it did moisten through all my clothes." Up and down he estimated this hill at six miles, " the way so uneven, stoney, and full of bogs, quagmires, and long heath, that a dog with three legs would there outrun a horse with four." At night, "with extreme travail," he came to the place where he could see the Brae of Marr, " which is a large country, all composed of such mountains, that Shooter's Hill, Gad's Hill, Highgate Hill, Hampstead Hill, Birdtop Hill, or Malvern Hills, are but mole-hills in comparison, or like a liver or gizzard under a capon's wing, in respect of the altitude of their tops, or perpendicularity of their bottoms."

Here he found his friends, with lords and ladies, and hundreds of knights, esquires, and followers, all in one habit, " as if Lycurgus had been there, and made laws of equality; for at this annual hunting, every one conformed to the habit of the highlandmen, who for the most part speak nothing but Irish, and in former times were those people which were called the Red-Shanks. Their habit is shoes with but one sole a-piece, stockings which they call short-hose, made of a warm stuff of divers colours, which they call tartane; as for breeches, many of them nor their forefathers, never wore any, but a jerkin of the same stuff that their hose is of, their garters being bands or wreathes of hay or straw, with a plaid about their shoulders, which is a mantle of divers colours, much finer and lighter stuff than their hose, with blue flat caps on their heads, a handkerchief knit with two knots about their necks, and thus were they attired. Now their weapons are long bows and forked arrows, swords and targets, harquebusses, muskets, dirks, and Loquhabor-axes; with these arms I found many of them armed for the hunting. As for their attire, any man of what degree soever, that comes amongst them, must not disdain to wear it; for if they do, then they will disdain to hunt, or willingly to bring on their dogs: but if men be kind unto them and be in their habit, then are they conquered with kindness, and the sport will be plentiful." The Earl of Marr put the Water-Poet "into this shape," and after leaving his house he was twelve days "before he saw either house, corn-field, or habitation for any creature but deer, wild horses, wolves, and such like." There were, however, " small cottages built on purpose to lodge in, which they call Lonquhards."

Taylor fared plentifully at this noble hunting, and entered heartily into the sport.

" I thank my good Lord Erskin, he commanded that I should always be lodged in his lodging, the kitchen being always on the side of a bank, many kettles and pots boiling, and many spits turning and winding, with great variety of cheer: as venison baked, sodden, roast and stewed; beef, mutton, goats, kid, hares, fresh salmon, pidgeons, hens, capons, chickens, partridges, moorecoots, heathcocks, caperkellies, and termagants; good ale, sack, white, and claret, tent, (or allegant,) with most potent aquavitæ. All these, and more than these we had continually, in superfluous abundance, caught by falconers, fowlers, fishers, and brought by my lord's tenants and purveyors to victual our camp, which consisteth of fourteen or fifteen hundred men and horses. The manner of the hunting is this: five or six hundred men do rise early in the morning, and they do disperse themselves divers ways, and seven, eight, or ten miles compass, they do bring or chase in the deer in many herds, (two, three, or four hundred in a herd,) to such and such a place, as the noblemen shall appoint them; then when day is come, the lords and gentlemen of their companies do ride or go to the said places, sometimes wading up to the middle through bournes and rivers: and then they being come to the place, do lie down on the ground till those foresaid scouts, which are called the Tinckhell, do bring down the deer. But as the proverb says of a bad cook, so these Tinckhell men do like their own fingers; for besides their bows and arrows, which they carry with them, we can hear now and then an arquebuss or a musket go off, which they do seldom discharge in vain: then after we had stayed there three hours or thereabouts, we might perceive the deer appear on the hills round about us, (their heads making a show like a wood,) which being followed close by the Tinckhell, are chased down into the valley where we lay; then all the valley on each side being waylaid with a hundred couple of strong Irish greyhounds, they are let loose as occasion serves upon the herd of deer, that with dogs, guns, arrows, dirks, and daggers, in the space of two hours, fourscore fat deer were slain; which after are disposed of, some one way and some another, twenty and thirty miles, and more than enough left for us to make merry withal at our rendezvous. I liked the sport so well, that I made these two sonnets following.

". Why should I waste invention, to endite
  Ovidian fictions, or Olympian games?
  My misty muse enlightened with more light,
  To a more noble pitch her aim she frames.
  I must relate to my great master, James,
  The Caledonian annual peaceful war;
  How noble minds do eternize their fames,
  By martial meeting in the Brae of Marr:
  How thousand gallant spirits came near and far,
  With swords and targets, arrows, bows, and guns,
  That all the troop, to men of judgement, are
  The God of War's great never conquered sons.
  The sport is manly, yet none bleed but beasts,
  And last the victor on the vanquished feasts.

  If sport like this can on the mountains be,
  Where Phœbus' flames can never melt the snow,
  Then let who list delight in vales below;
  Sky-kissing mountains pleasure are for me:
  What braver object can man's eye-sight see,
  Than noble, worshipful, and worthy wights,
  As if they were prepared for sundry fights,
  Yet all in sweet society agree?
  Through heather, moss, 'mongst frogs and bogs and
      fogs,
  'Mongst craggy cliffs and thunder-battered hills,

Hares, hinds, bucks, roes, are chased by men and
    dogs,
Where two hours' hunting fourscore fat deer kills.
Lowland, your sports are low as is your seat!
The highland games and minds are high and great."

"Being come to our lodgings, there was such baking, boiling, roasting, and stewing, as if Cook Ruffian had been there to have scalded the devil in his feathers: and after supper a fire of fir-wood as high as an indifferent may-pole; for I assure you, that the Earl of Marr will give any man that is his friend, for thanks, as many fir-trees (that are as good as any ship's masts in England) as are worth (if they were in any place near the Thames, or any other portable river) the best earldom in England or Scotland either; for I dare affirm, he hath as many growing there, as would serve for masts (from this time to the end of the world) for all the ships, caracks, hoyes, galleys, boats, drumlers, barks, and water-crafts, that are now or can be in the world these forty years."

After the hunt broke up he was entertained at Ruthen by the Lord of Engie, at Ballo Castle by the Laird of Graunt, at Tarnaway by the Earl of Murray, at Spinaye by the Bishop of Murray; and by the Marquis of Huntley, at a sumptuous house of his, named the Bog of Geethe. And after five-and thirty days' hunting and travelling, he returned to Edinburgh, those lords giving him gold to defray his charges on the journey. He stayed at Edinburgh eight days, to recover "from falls and bruises received in the highland mountainous hunting." Many worthy gentlemen there suffered him neither to want wine nor good cheer. "At Leith," he says, "I found my long approved and assured good friend, Master Benjamin Johnson, at one Master John Stuart's house. I thank him for his great kindness towards me, for at my taking leave of him, he gave me a piece of gold of two-and-twenty shillings to drink his health in England, and, withal, willed me to remember his kind commendation to all his friends. So with a friendly farewell I left him, as well as I hope never to see him in a worse estate; for he is amongst noblemen and gentlemen, that know his true worth and their honour, where with much respect and love he is worthily entertained."

Being now to commence his journey home, according to the bond, he discharged his pockets of all the money he had at the port or gate called the Netherbows, and as he came pennyless within the walls, went moneyless out of them. But he had no meagre days, nor bivouacking at nights, on his homeward road; for Master James Acmooty, with whom he presently fell in, was going to London, and for the sake of his company undertook that neither he nor his horse should want upon the way; an undeserved courtesy, of which Taylor says, his want persuaded his manners to accept; not that he availed himself of it on the whole journey, for he overtook other friends at Newcastle, where Sir Henry Witherington gave him a bay mare, (because he would accept no money,) in requital for the loaf; he tried his own fortune from Topcliffe to York, and obtained letters for the rest of the way, or found acquaintance. His friends came to meet him at Islington, at the sign of the Maidenhead, when with all love he was entertained with much good cheer, and after supper they had a play of the Life and Death of Guy of Warwick, played by the Earl of Derby's men, and on the next morning, Oct. 15, he came to his house at London.

> "Thus did I neither spend, or beg, or ask,
> By any course, direct or indirectly;
> But in each tittle I performed my task
> According to my bill most circumspectly."

His next journey, which was also undertaken as a wagering adventure, was to Prague, in the year 1620. He published an account of it, *more suo*, in prose and verse. "The truth," he says, "is, that I did chiefly write it, because I am of much acquaintance, and cannot pass the streets but I am continually stayed by one or other, to know what news; so that sometimes I am four hours before I can go the length of two pair of buts, where such nonsense or senseless questions are propounded to me, that calls many seeming wise men's wisdom in question, drawing aside the curtains of their understandings, and laying their ignorance wide open. First, John Easy takes me, and holds me fast by the fist half an hour; and will needs torture some news out of me from Spinola, whom I was never near by five hundred miles, for he is in the Palatinate country and I was in Bohemia. I am no sooner eased of him, but Gregory Gandergoose, an alderman of Gotham, catches me by the goll, demanding if Bohemia be a great town, and whether there be any meat in it, and whether the last fleet of ships be arrived there." (You know, reader, that Prague might have been a sea-port, according to Corporal Trim.) "His mouth being stopt, a third examines me boldly what news from Vienna?

where the Emperor's army is, and what the Duke of Bavaria doth? what is become of Count Buquoy? how fare all the Englishmen? where lies the King of Bohemia's forces? what Bethlem Gabor doth? what tidings of Dampeier? and such a tempest of inquisitions that almost shakes my patience in pieces. To ease myself of all which, I was enforced to set pen to paper and let this poor pamphlet (my herald, or *nuntius,*) travel and talk, while I take my ease with silence.

The Queen of Bohemia, who was then such in possession, and not in title alone, made him a partaker of her bounty at Prague; and he had her youngest son, Prince Rupert, in his arms, and brought away, to keep as a memorial of this honour, the infant's shoes.

" Lambskin they were, as white as innocence,
   (True patterns for the footsteps of a Prince,)
   And time will come, as I do hope in God,
   He that in childhood with these shoes was shod,
   Shall with his manly feet once trample down
   All Antichristian foes to his renown."

Poor Taylor lived to see the prince employed in a very different war from what these lines anticipated!

Two years after this journey he made "a very

merry wherry-ferry voyage from London to York." Being forced by stress of weather to land at Cromer, the whole town was alarmed, he and his four men were supposed to be pirates, the constables took them into custody, and guards were set upon their wherry.

> "They did examine me, I answered then,
> I was John Taylor, and a waterman,
> And that my honest fellow Job, and I,
> Were servants to King James's Majesty;
> How we to York upon a mart were bound,
> And that we landed fearing to be drown'd.
> When all this would not satisfy the crew,
> I freely ope'd my trunks, and bade them view.
> I showed them Books of Chronicles and Kings,
> Some prose, some verse, some idle sonnetings;
> I showed them all my letters to the full.
> Some to York's Archbishop, and some to Hull."

Nothing, however, would satisfy the people, till two magistrates, (Sir Austin Palgrave and Mr. Robert Kempe,) had examined these invaders. These gentlemen knew the Water-Poet by name, and had read some of his books; they administered the oath of allegiance to him and his men, to content the people, and gave him "corn and wine and lodging too;" and he met then with as much assistance from the sailors there, as he had found incivility at first. He crossed the Wash with some danger, not knowing the place and having no pilot, and being caught in the Hyger. When he reached Boston he was glad to learn that the remainder of of his way might be performed by an inland navigation. Accordingly, he went up the Witham, fifty miles, to Lincoln, performing the distance in one day.

" From thence we passed a ditch of weeds and mud,
Which they do (falsely) there call Forcedike Flood,
For I'll be sworn no flood I could find there,
But dirt and filth which scarce my boat would bear:
'Tis eight miles long, and there our pains was such,
As all our travel did not seem so much.
My men did wade, and draw the boat like horses,
And scarce could tug her on with all our forces:
Moil'd, toil'd, mired, tired, still labouring, ever doing,
Yet were we nine long hours that eight miles going.
At last when as the day was well nigh spent,
We got from Forcedike's floodless flood to Trent."

Down the Trent then they proceeded to Gainsborough, which they reached just " as the windows of the day did shut;" and the next day entered the Humber, but instead of bending their course directly for York, they went out of it to touch at

Hull, and had nearly been swamped on the way, an east wind raising such waves against a swift ebb tide, that he had never seen any thing like it before in the course of his waterman's life.

He had letters to the mayor and other members of the corporation, as well as to private individuals, who were requested to make him welcome, and give him Hull cheese, which he says, " is much like a loaf out of a brewer's basket; for it is composed of two simples, malt and water, in one compound, and is cousin-german to the mightiest ale in England." Hops not being mentioned in this compound, it seems that the distinction between ale and beer continued to be known in his time. Here he was received not merely like a man whose company was acceptable to every one who could obtain it, but as a person, also, whose visit did honour to the town. Mayor and Aldermen entertained him, and he was pleased, as well he might, with the prosperity and good order of a place, where relief was provided for all the helpless poor and work for all the rest.

" Thanks, Mr. Mayor, for my bacon-gammon!
Thanks, Roger Parker, for my small fresh salmon!
'Twas excellent good; and more the truth to tell ye,
Boil'd with a fine plum-pudding in the belly.

"The sixth of August, well accompanied
With best of townsmen to the water-side,
There did I take my leave, and to my ship
I with my drum and colours quickly skip:
The one did dub-a-dub, and rumble brave,
The ensign in the air did play and wave;
I launch'd, supposing all things had been done;
Bounce, from the Blockhouse, quoth a roaring gun;
And waving hats on both sides, with content,
I cried adieu! adieu! and thence we went."

That night he got to Cawood, and called the next day on the good old archbishop, Tobias Matthew, who gave him gold and made him dine at his own table, while his men made good cheer in the hall. After dinner they proceeded to York, so finishing their adventure. He offered the boat, as in duty bound, he says, to the Lord Mayor, who after some deliberation declined the present. Taylor, therefore, found a purchaser for it. From the Mayor he got nothing but a cup of claret and some beer. He says,

"I gave his lordship, in red gilded leather,
A well-bound book of all my works together,
Which he did take.——

" Here I make a full point, for I received not a

point in exchange." He then returned to London by land, and his Epilogue says,

"Thus have I brought to end a work of pain,
I wish it may requite me with some gain;
For well I wot the dangers where I ventured,
No full-bagg'd man would ever durst have entered."

In the ensuing year (1623) he made a similar voyage from London to Christ Church, in Hampshire, and so up the Avon to Salisbury, and this was "for toyle, travail, and danger," the worst and most difficult passage he had yet made. These desperate adventures did not answer the purpose for which they were undertaken, and he complains of this in what he calls (*Taylorice*) the Scourge of Baseness, a Kicksey Winsey, or a Lerry-Come-Twang.

"I made my journey for no other ends
But to get money and to try my friends.—
They took a book worth twelve pence, and were bound
To give a crown, an angel, or a pound,
A noble, piece, or half-piece,—what they list:
They past their words, or freely set their fist.
Thus got I sixteen hundred hands and fifty,
Which sum I did suppose was somewhat thrifty;
And now my youths with shifts and tricks and cavils,
Above seven hundred, play the sharking javils."

Four thousand and five hundred books he had given out, he says, upon these implied or expressed conditions; they had cost him more than seven-score pounds, and his Scotch walk had been sport to the trouble of vainly tramping about in seeking what was his due. He had given out money as well as books. The censures which were past upon him, and others, who like him went dangerous voyages by sea in small wherries, for "tempting God by undertaking such perilous courses," he acknowledges were not undeserved, and said that in this way he had done his last. Yet, it appears, that after this he engaged in a more desperate adventure than any of the former, that of going from London to Queenborough in a paper boat, with two stock-fish tied to two canes for oars! Roger Bird, a vintner, was the principal in this mad enterprize. They took with them eight large and well-blown bladders, which were found necessary in the course of half an hour; for before they had got three miles, the paper bottom fell to pieces, and they had only the skeleton of the boat to trust to, and their bladders, four on each side. There they sat, "within six inches of the brim."

"Thousands of people all the shores did hide,
And thousands more did meet us on the tide,

With scullers, oars, with ship-boats and with barges,
To gaze on us they put themselves to charges.
Thus did we drive, and drive the time away,
Till pitchy night had driven away the day.
The sun unto the under world was fled,
The moon was loth to rise, and kept her bed;
The stars did twinkle, but the ebon clouds
Their light, our sight, obscures and overshrouds.
The tossing billows made our boat to caper,
Our paper form scarce being form of paper;
The water four miles broad, no oars to row;
Night dark, and where we were we did not know:
And thus 'twixt doubt and fear, hope and despair,
I fell to work, and Roger Bird to prayer;
And as the surges up and down did heave us,
He cried most fervently, good Lord, receive us!"

Taylor tells us, honestly, that he prayed as much, but he worked at the same time, which the poor wineman was not waterman enough to do: and having been on the water from Saturday, "at evening tide," till Monday morning, they reached Queenborough; and he says, being

———————————— " aland,
I took my fellow Roger by the hand,
And both of us, ere we two steps did go,
Gave thanks to God that had preserved us so;
Confessing that his mercy us protected,
When as we least deserved, and less expected."

They arrived on the fair day, when the mayor entertained all comers with bread, beer, and oysters. They presented him with the skeleton of their boat, which

>   ——— " to glorify that town of Kent,
> He meant to hang up for a monument;"

but while he was feasting them, the country people tore it piecemeal, every man wishing to carry away a scrap as a memorial of this mad adventure.

Taylor was engaged in a *flyting* with Fennor, who seems to have been a rival of his own rank: the fashion of such contests in ribaldry prevailed a little before his time in France and in Scotland; our literature has luckily escaped it, at least, I know not of any other example than the present. The circumstances which gave rise to it are related by the Water Poet, " to any that can read," in a short epistle prefixed to " Taylor's Revenge, or the Rhymer, William Fennor, firkt, ferreted, and finely fetcht over the coals." " Be it," he says, " known unto all men, that I, John Taylor, waterman, did agree with William Fennor, (who arrogantly and falsely entitles himself the King's Majesty's Rhyming Poet,) to answer me at a trial of wit, on the seventh of October last, (1614,) on the Hope stage, on the Bankside; and the said Fennor received of me ten shillings in earnest of his coming to meet me; whereupon I caused a thousand bills to be printed, and divulged my name a thousand ways and more, giving my friends and divers of my acquaintance notice of this Bear-Garden banquet of dainty conceits; and when the day came that the play should have been performed, the house being filled with a great audience, who had all spent their monies extraordinarily, then this companion for an ass ran away, and left me for a fool, amongst thousands of critical conjurors, where I was ill thought of by my friends, scorned by my foes; and in conclusion, in a greater puzzle than the blind bear in the midst of all her whip-broth. Besides the sum of twenty pounds in money, I lost my reputation amongst many, and gained disgrace instead of my better expectations. In revenge of which wrongs done unto me by the said rhyming rascal, I have written this invective against him; chiefly because the ill-looking hound doth not confess he hath injured me; nor hath not so much honesty as to bring or send me my money that he took for earnest of me, but on the contrary part, he rails and abuses me with his calumnious tongue, and scandalizes me in all companies where he hears me nominated."

The price of admission had been raised upon this occasion, and when the audience had exhausted their patience in waiting for Fennor, they vented their indignation upon Taylor, pelting as well as abusing him, with that cowardly brutality of which all mobs seem capable. The Water Poet in return sent out a volley of vituperative verse both against them and the defaulter; and in the collected volume of his works, he was just enough to insert Fennor's defence, " wherein the Waterman, John Taylor, is dasht, sowst, and finally fallen into the Thames, with his slanderous taxation, base imputations, scandalous accusations, and foul abominations, against his Majesty's Rhyming Poet." From this answer it appears that Fennor, who had obtained reputation enough as an improvisatore to exhibit before James I., had assented to Taylor's project, which was that they should perform a sort of drama between them, Taylor having " studied several humours in prose," and Fennor being to play his part extemporaneously in verse; for which he required either " half the commodity thereof; or security for five pounds; or else twenty shillings in hand, and the rest as the day afforded." He excused himself for his non-appearance by a lame story, and poured out a volley of recriminative ribaldry, which the Water Poet answered in the same strain. The common estimate of Taylor's writings seems to have been taken from these pieces, which are the worst, and from his Rhymed Chronicles, which are the most worthless of his productions.

He was a married man, and the ensuing lines may show that he " never accounted his marriage among his infelicities:"

" I have a wife which I was wont to praise,
But that was in my younger wooing days:
And though she's neither shrew, nor sheep, I vow,
With justice I cannot dispraise her now.
She hath an instrument that's ever strung
To exercise my patience on—her tongue:
But past all question, and beyond all doubt,
She'll ne'er infect my forehead with the gout.
A married man, some say, hath two days gladness,
And all his life else is a lingering sadness;
The one day's mirth is, when he first is married,
The other's when his wife's to burying carried:
One I have had, should I the t'other see,
It could not be a day of mirth to me,
For I, (as many have,) when I did woo,
Myself in tying fast did not undo;

"But I have by my long experience found
I had been undone, had I not been bound.
I have my bonds of marriage long enjoyed,
And do not wish my obligation void."

When the troubles came on, the Water Poet, who had often tasted of the royal bounty, was too honest and too brave a man to turn with the tide; he left London, therefore, and retired to Oxford. He had formerly found shelter there during a plague, an account of which he published and dated from Oriel College. In one of his tracts he acknowledges that the very air of the colleges and schools, the books he had read there, and the dictionaries he had pored upon, had much "illustrated, elevated, and illuminated his intellect;" for he had "picked out here and there etymologies, expressions, explanations, and significations of hard words out of divers tongues." He now opened a victualling house there, and employed his pen against the Roundheads, and made himself, it is said, "much esteemed for his facetious company." Upon the surrender of Oxford and the ruin of the royal cause, he returned to Westminster, and kept a public house in Phœnix Alley, near Long Acre, where, after the King's death, he set up a Mourning Crown for his sign. This, however, he found it necessary to remove, and then he hung up his own portrait in its stead. His health and spirits he retained to a good old age, and when more than seventy made a journey through Wales, in the year 1652, and published an account of it. Two years afterwards he died, at the age of seventy-four, and was buried in the church-yard of St. Paul's, Covent Garden.

An epitaph was composed upon him somewhat in his own style:

"Here lies the Water Poet, honest John,
Who rowed in the streams of Helicon;
Where having many rocks and dangers past,
He at the haven of Heaven arrived at last."

There is a portrait of him bearing date 1655, by his nephew, who was a painter at Oxford, and presented it to the Bodleian, where it was thought not unworthy of a place. He is represented in a black scull-cap, and black gown or rather cloak. The countenance is described to me as one of "well-fed rotundity; the eyes small, with an expression of cunning, into which their natural shrewdness had probably been deteriorated by the painter; their colour seems to have been hazel:

there is scarcely any appearance of eye-brows; the lips have a slight cast of playfulness or satire. The brow is wrinkled, and he is in the fashion of mustachios with a tuft of beard under the lip. The portrait now is, like the building in which it has thus long been preserved, in a state of rapid decay:" " I hope," says the friend to whom I am obliged for this account of it, " his verse is of a more durable quality:—for *ut pictura poësis* would annihilate him altogether."

> " All making, marring, never-turning Time,
> To all that is, is period and is prime;
> Time wears out Fortune, Love, and Death, and Fame."

So sung the Water Poet;—it wore out him, and is now wearing out his picture and his works; and he is not one of those writers for whom a palingenesia can be expected from their dust. Yet we have lately seen the whole of Herrick's poems republished, a coarse-minded and beastly writer, whose dunghill, when the few flowers that grew therein had been transplanted, ought never to have been disturbed. Those flowers indeed are beautiful and perennial; but they should have been removed from the filth and ordure in which they are embedded. There is nothing of John Taylor's which deserves preservation for its intrinsic merit alone, but in the collection of his pieces which I have perused there is a great deal to illustrate the manners of his age; and as he lived more than twenty years after this collection was printed, and continued publishing till the last, there is probably much in his uncollected works also which for the same reason ought to be preserved. A curious and useful volume of selections might be formed from them. There are many perishing writers from whose otherwise worthless works it is much to be desired that excerpts of this kind should be made: a series of such would be not less valuable than the Harleian Miscellany or the Somers Tracts.

If the Water Poet had been in a higher grade of society, and bred to some regular profession, he would probably have been a much less distinguished person in his generation. No spoon could have suited his mouth so well as the wooden one to which he was born. His way of life was best suited to his character, nor could any regular education so fully have brought out the sort of talent which he possessed. Fortunately, also, he came into the world at the right time, and lived in an age when Kings and Queens condescended to notice him, nobles and archbishops admitted him to their table, and mayors and corporations received him with civic honours. The next of our uneducated poets was composed of very different clay,—and did not moisten it so well.

STEPHEN DUCK.

STEPHEN DUCK was born at Great Charlton, a little village in Wiltshire, in the beginning of the last century. His parents were in the lowest rank of life; and as it was his hard hap to be complained of by the village schoolmaster for " taking his learning too fast, even faster than it could be bestowed upon him," his poor mother took him from school and set him to the plough, " lest he should become too fine a gentleman for the family that produced him." He was a boy who, in old times, would have been noticed by the monks of the nearest monastery—would then have made his way to Oxford, or perhaps to Paris, as a begging scholar—have risen to be a bishop or mitred abbot—have done honour to his station, and have left behind him good works and a good name. In his own days, if he had met with timely patronage enough to have placed him at an endowed grammar school, as fair a career might have been opened to him in our Established Church; for he would have deserved its honours, and some of its honours have always been awarded to desert, even in the worst times.

Being from his fourteenth year wholly engaged in the lowest and hardest employments of a country life, Stephen forgot almost all the little arithmetic he had learnt at school, and this made him uneasy, for " he had a certain longing after knowledge." That uneasiness, however, was suspended by his longing for a wife also: it returned upon him, after an early marriage, when he had no time to spare, no books, and no money wherewith to purchase any. But in this case also love will find a way; he worked extra hours, and so obtained extra payment, which having so earned he might fairly appropriate to the meritorious object of improving himself. So he bought first a book of vulgar arithmetic, then one of decimals, and a third upon mensuration; and these he studied in those hours which could be spared from sleep, after the labours of the day.

It appears that he met with little encouragement for his intellectual ambition from his wife, nor was it likely that he should. But by good fortune one of his acquaintance, who had been two or three years in service at London, came to reside at

Charlton, and brought with him a few books, which, being fond of reading, he had purchased in the great city. With him Stephen became intimate, and they used to read together, and talk over the points which they were thus led to think on. This was the greatest happiness of his life. "Their minds," says Spence, "were their own, neither improved nor spoiled by laying in a stock of learning. They were, perhaps, equally well inclined to learn; both struggling for a little knowledge; and like a couple of rowers on the same bottom, while they were only striving perhaps which should outdo his companion, they were really each helping the other, and driving the boat on the faster.

"Perhaps you would be willing to know what books their little library consisted of. Milton, the Spectator, and Seneca, were his first favourites; Telemachus, with another piece by the same hand, (the Demonstration of the Being of a God,) and Addison's Defence of Christianity, his next. They had an English Dictionary, and a sort of English Grammar; an Ovid, of long standing with them, and a Bysshe's Art of Poetry, of later acquisition; Seneca's Morals made the name of L'Estrange dear to them; and, as I imagine, might occasion their getting his Josephus, in folio, which was the largest purchase in their collection. They had one volume of Shakespeare with seven of his plays in it. Besides these, Stephen had read three or four other plays; some of Epictetus, Waller, Dryden's Virgil, Prior, Hudibras, Tom Brown, and the London Spy. With these helps," continues Spence, " Stephen is grown something of a poet and something of a philosopher. I find by him, that from his infancy he has had a cast in his mind towards poetry. He has delighted, as far back as he can remember, in verses and in singing. He speaks of strange emotions that he has felt on the top-performances of the little choir of songsters in a country chancel; and mentions his first hearing of an organ as a remarkable epocha of his life. He seems to be a pretty good judge too of a musical line; but I imagine that he does not hear verses in his mind as he repeats them. I don't know whether you understand me, I mean that his ideas of notes in a verse, and his manner of repeating the same verse, are often different. For he points out an harmonious line well enough, and yet he generally spoils its harmony by his way of speaking it."

Paradise Lost carried with it no doubt a strong recommendation in its subject, but it perplexed him, and he read it twice or thrice with a Dictionary, tudying it, as a studious youth goes through a Greek or Latin author. The Spectator, too, which he said improved his understanding more than any thing, taught him to appreciate some of the merits of that poem, and Spence says he could point out particular beauties which it required " a good keen eye to discover." He frequently took a volume of the Spectator with him to his work, and laboured harder than any one else, like a man engaged to work by the piece, that he might honestly get half an hour for reading one of the numbers; but by sitting down at such times incautiously in the sweat of his brow, he injured his health. The poems which he now and then met with in the Spectator " helped on his natural bent that way, and made him willing to try whether he could not do something in the same kind himself. This he could do while he was at work; and he pleased himself so well that at last he began to venture these thoughts on paper. What he did of this kind was very inconsiderable; only scattered thoughts, and generally not above four or five lines on the same subject; which, as there was nobody thereabouts that cared for verses, nor any body that could tell him whether they were good or bad, he generally flung into the fire as soon as he had pleased himself enough in reading them."

But though Stephen was too conscientious to neglect his work at any time for his studies, and consequently never gave his master cause for complaint, he was not so fortunate at home, where he had a person less considerate, if not less reasonable, to deal with. It was his lot at this time to be duck-peck'd by his lawful wife, who held herself to be lawful mistress also, and told all the neighbourhood that her husband dealt with the devil, or was going mad, for he did nothing but talk to himself and tell his fingers. Probably she acquitted the devil of any share in her husband's aberrations, and became reconciled to his conduct when she found that he began to be favourably noticed by persons in a higher station. The country people, who had long talked of him as a scholar, began now to report that he could make verses, which was yet more surprising, according to their notions: a young Oxonian, Stanley by name, hearing this, sent for Stephen, and was so well satisfied with his conversation, as to desire that he would write him a letter in verse. He had never written what Spence calls a whole copy of verses before; but he now produced about fifty lines, of which the beginning is a fair specimen.

"Sir,
I have, before the time prescribed by you,
Exposed my weak production to your view;
Which may, I hope, have pardon at your hand,
Because produced to light by your command.
Perhaps you might expect some finished ode,
Or sacred song to sound the praise of God;
A glorious thought, and laudable! But then,
Think what illiterate poet guides the pen.
Ill suit such tasks with one who holds the plough;
Such lofty subjects with a fate so low."

These verses were shown to some of the neighbouring clergymen, and they, having inquired into his character and talked with him, encouraged him to go on, "and gave him some presents, which, as things stood then, were a great help to him." He then put together and completed some verses which he had commenced on Poverty. To Poverty, as his acquaintance and familiar guest, he says,

—————— "Thou art no formidable foe,
Except to little souls who think thee so:"

and after comparing the good and evil of affluent

circumstances and of narrow ones, he concludes thus:—

"Since wealth can never make the vicious blest,
Nor poverty subdue the virtuous breast:
Since both from Heaven's unerring hand are sent,
LORD! give me either, give me but content."

Stephen's had been a wholesome course of reading; though he had taken some pleasure in Tom Brown's Letters from the Dead, and the London Spy, he " did not much care to look into them," he said, after he became acquainted with the Spectator: he liked what little he had read of Epictetus, " but 'twas Seneca that had made him happy in his own mind." The gentlemen of the country began to notice him now, and the little presents he received from them " made him quite easy as to his circumstances." The only thing that he was then solicitous about, was how he might succeed as to the poetry he should be employed in; this was his chief concern. But even this seemed to proceed not so much from any desire of fame as from a principle of gratitude; or, as he expressed it, his longing to please those friends that had been so generous to him.

Mr. Stanley, who was now in holy orders, gave

him for a subject of his next poem, his own way of life, and showed his own judgment in so doing. Stephen, accordingly, composed the Thresher's Labour, which, in the collection of his pieces, is inscribed to his first patron. The picture of rural occupations, here drawn from the life, is very different from what we find in pastorals; but the truth of the description is not its only merit, for there are passages in it which would have done no discredit to more celebrated names.

" Soon as the golden harvest quits the plain,
 And Ceres' gifts reward the farmer's pain,
 What corn each sheaf will yield, intent to hear,
 And guess from thence the profits of the year,
 He calls his reapers forth: around we stand
 With deep attention, waiting his command.
 To each our task he readily divides,
 And pointing to our different stations guides;
 As he directs, to distant barns we go,
 Here two for wheat, and there for barley two.
 But first to show what he expects to find,
 These words, or words like these, disclose his mind:
 " So dry the corn was carried from the field,
 So easily 'twill thresh, so well 'twill yield,
 Sure large day's-works I well may hope for now.
 Come, strip and try; let's see what you can do!"

Divested of our cloaths, with flail in hand,
At proper distance, front to front we stand.
And first the threshal's gently swung, to prove
Whether with just exactness it will move:
That once secure, we swiftly whirl them round,
From the strong planks our crab-tree staves rebound,
And echoing barns return the rattling sound.
Now in the air our knotty weapons fly,
And now with equal force descend from high;
Down one, one up, so well they keep the time,
The Cyclops' hammers could not truer chime;
Nor with more heavy strokes could Etna groan,
When Vulcan forged the arms for Thetis' son.
In briny streams our sweat descends apace,
Drops from our locks, or trickles down our face.
No intermission in our work we know;
The noisy threshal must for ever go.
Their master absent, others safely play,
The sleeping threshal does itself betray."

* * * * *

" Our eye beholds no pleasing object here,
No chearful sound diverts our listening ear.
The shepherd well may tune his voice to sing,
Inspired with all the beauties of the spring.
No fountains murmur here, no lambkins play,
No linnets warble, and no fields look gay;
'Tis all a gloomy, melancholy scene,
Fit only to provoke the Muse's spleen.

When sooty pease we thresh, you scarce can know
Our native colour, as from work we go:
The sweat, the dust, and suffocating smoke,
Make us so much like Ethiopians look,
We scare our wives, when evening brings us home,
And frighted infants think the bugbear come.
Week after week we this dull task pursue,
Unless when winnowing days produce a new:
A new, indeed, but frequently a worse!
The threshal yields but to the master's curse.
He counts the bushels, counts how much a-day,
Then swears we've idled half our time away;
' Why look ye, rogues, d'ye think that this will do?
Your neighbours thresh as much again as you.' "

From this winter and spring work Stephen passes to his summer occupations.

" Before the door our welcome master stands,
Tells us the ripen'd grass requires our hands.
The grateful tiding presently imparts
Life to our looks, and spirits to our hearts.
We wish the happy season may be fair;
And, joyful, long to breathe in opener air.
This change of labour seems to give such ease,
With thoughts of happiness ourselves we please.
But, ah! how rarely's happiness complete!
There's always bitter mingled with the sweet.
When first the lark sings prologue to the day,
We rise, admonish'd by his early lay;

This new employ with eager haste to prove,
This new employ, becomes so much our love.
Alas! that human joys shou'd change so soon!
Our morning pleasure turns to pain at noon.
The birds salute us as to work we go,
And with new life our bosoms seem to glow.
On our right shoulder hangs the crooked blade,
The weapon destined to uncloath the mead:
Our left supports the whetstone, scrip, and beer,
This for our scythes, and these ourselves to cheer.
And now the field designed to try our might
At length appears and meets our longing sight.
The grass and ground we view with careful eyes,
To see which way the best advantage lies;
And, hero-like, each claims the foremost place.
At first our labour seems a sportive race:
With rapid force our sharpen'd blades we drive,
Strain every nerve, and blow for blow we give.
All strive to vanquish, tho' the victor gains
No other glory but the greatest pains.
But when the scorching sun is mounted high,
And no kind barns with friendly shade are nigh,
Our weary scythes entangle in the grass,
While streams of sweat run trickling down apace;
Our sportive labour we too late lament,
And wish that strength again we vainly spent."

* * * * *

"With heat and labour tir'd, our scythes we quit,
Search out a shady tree, and down we sit:

From scrip and bottle hope new strength to gain;
But scrip and bottle too are tried in vain.
Down our parch'd throats we scarce the bread can get,
And, quite o'erspent with toil, but faintly eat;
Nor can the bottle only answer all;
The bottle and the beer are both too small.
Time flows: again we rise from off the grass;
Again each mower takes his proper place;
Not eager now, as late, our strength to prove,
But all contented regular to move.
We often whet, and often view the sun;
As often wish his tedious race was run.
At length he veils his purple face from sight,
And bids the weary labourer good night.
Homewards we move, but spent so much with toil,
We slowly walk and rest at every stile.
Our good expecting wives, who think we stay,
Got to the door, soon eye us in the way.
Then from the pot the dumplin's catch'd in haste,
And homely by its side the bacon placed;
Supper and sleep by morn new strength supply,
And out we set again, our work to try;
But not so early quite, nor quite so fast,
As to our cost we did the morning past.
Soon as the rising sun has drank the dew,
Another scene is open to our view:
Our master comes, and at his heels a throng
Of prattling females, arm'd with rake and prong;

Prepar'd, whilst he is here, to make his hay,
Or, if he turns his back, prepared to play;
But here, or gone, sure of this comfort still;
Here's company, so they may chat their fill.
Ah! were their hands so active as their tongues,
How nimbly then would move the rakes and prongs!

" The grass again is spread upon the ground,
Till not a vacant place is to be found;
And while the parching sun-beams on it shine,
The haymakers have time allowed to dine;
That soon dispatched, they still sit on the ground,
And the brisk chat, renew'd, afresh goes round.
All talk at once; but seeming all to fear,
That what they speak the rest will hardly hear;
Till by degrees so high their notes they strain,
A stander-by can nought distinguish plain.
So loud's their speech, and so confused their noise,
Scarce puzzled Echo can return the voice.
Yet spite of this, they bravely all go on;
Each scorns to be, or seem to be, outdone.
Meanwhile the changing sky begins to lour,
And hollow winds proclaim a sudden shower;
The tattling crowd can scarce their garments gain,
Before descends the thick impetuous rain;
Their noisy prattle all at once is done,
And to the hedge they soon for shelter run.

" Thus have I seen, on a bright summer's day,
On some green brake, a flock of sparrows play;

From twig to twig, from bush to bush they fly,
And with continued chirping fill the sky;
But on a sudden, if a storm appears,
Their chirping noise no longer dins our ears;
They fly for shelter to the thickest bush;
There silent sit, and all at once is hush.

" But better fate succeeds this rainy day,
And little labour serves to make the hay.
Fast as 'tis cut, so kindly shines the sun,
Turn'd once or twice, the pleasing work is done.
Next day the cocks appear in equal rows,
Which the glad master in safe ricks bestows.

" The spacious fields we now no longer range;
And yet, hard fate! still work for work we change.
Back to the barns we hastily are sent,
Where lately so much time we pensive spent;
Not pensive now, we bless the friendly shade;
And to avoid the parching sun are glad.
Yet little time we in the shade remain,
Before our master calls us forth again;
And says, ' for harvest now yourselves prepare;
The ripen'd harvest now demands your care.
Get all things ready, and be quickly drest:
Early next morn I shall disturb your rest.'
Strict to his word, for scarce the dawn appears,
Before his hasty summons fills our ears.
His hasty summons we obey, and rise,
While yet the stars are glimmering in the skies.

With him our guide, we to the wheat-field go,
He to appoint, and we the work to do.

" Ye reapers, cast your eyes around the field,
And view the various scenes its beauties yield;
Then look again with a more tender eye,
To think how soon it must in ruin lie!
For, once set in, where'er our blows we deal,
There's no resisting of the well-whet steel:
But here or there, where'er our course we bend,
Sure desolation does our steps attend.

" The morning past, we sweat beneath the sun,
And but uneasily our work goes on.
Before us we perplexing thistles find,
And corn blown adverse with the ruffling wind.
Behind, our master waits: and if he spies
One charitable ear, he grudging cries,
' Ye scatter half your wages o'er the land:'
Then scrapes the stubble with his greedy hand.

" Let those who feast at ease on dainty fare
Pity the reapers, who their feasts prepare:
For toils scarce ever ceasing press us now;
Rest never does but on the sabbath show;
And barely that our masters will allow.
Think what a painful life we daily lead;
Each morning early rise, go late to bed:
Nor when asleep are we secure from pain,
We then perform our labours o'er again:

Our mimic fancy ever restless seems,
And what we act awake she acts in dreams.
Hard fate! our labours even in sleep don't cease;
Scarce Hercules e'er felt such toils as these!

"But soon we rise the bearded crop again,
Soon Phœbus' rays well dry the golden grain.
Pleas'd with the scene, our master glows with joy,
Bids us for carrying all our force employ;
When straight, confusion o'er the field appears,
And stunning clamours fill the workmen's ears;
The bells and clashing whips alternate sound,
And rattling waggons thunder o'er the ground.
The wheat, when carry'd, pease, and other grain,
We soon secure, and leave a fruitless plain;
In noisy triumph the last load moves on,
And loud huzzas proclaim the harvest done.
Our master, joyful at the pleasing sight,
Invites us all to feast with him at night.
A table plentifully spread we find,
And jugs of humming ale to cheer the mind;
Which he, too generous, pushes round so fast,
We think no toil's to come, nor mind the past.
But the next morning soon reveals the cheat,
When the same toils we must again repeat;
To the same barns must back again return,
To labour there for room for next year's corn.

"Thus, as the year's revolving course goes round,
No respite from our labour can be found:

Like Sisyphus, our work is never done:
Continually rolls back the heavy stone.
New growing labours still succeed the past;
And growing always new, must always last."

This is the best specimen of Stephen Duck's productions in verse, and certainly the command of language and the skill in versification which it displays, manifest perseverance and ability which very well deserved the encouragement he met with. Mr. Stanley proposed to him, as a subject for his next attempt, the story of the Shunamite woman and her child, and this poem was thought by his patrons to be the best of his performances. He first wrote it in blank verse, but upon reading it over he found that the language was not sublime enough to sustain the metre, and therefore he recast it in rhyme; and though Milton was his favourite poet, he never again attempted what he had good sense enough to perceive he was incapable of performing as it ought to be done. "To know how much he deserves," says Spence, "one should converse with him, and hear on what reasons he omitted such a part; why he shortens his stile in this place, and enlarges in that; whence he has such a word, and whence such an idea." For Stephen made great use of his little reading, enriched his vocabulary by it, and imitated, yet not servilely, what might be adapted to his subject. He also planned his compositions, and " thought over all the parts, as he intended to arrange them, before he made the verses. For a poem of any length," the good poetry-professor remarks, " no doubt, 'tis as necessary to do this as it is to have a draft of a house before you go to building it; and yet, I believe, the common run of our poets have generally thought themselves above it, or never thought of it at all."

The Thresher now began to be so much talked of, that some knavish bookseller got together a collection of his verses, and published them for his own advantage, with what Stephen calls a very false account of the author, and a fictitious portrait of him, wherein he is represented with Milton in one hand and a flail in the other, coming from the barn towards a table, on which pen, ink, and paper are lying; pigs, poultry, and reapers, making up the rural accompaniments. But the Thresher's Labour had found its way to the Honourable Mrs. Clayton, a lady who was about the Queen's person; she showed it to the Queen, and Queen Caroline, with characteristic goodness, patronized the humble poet. He was invited to Windsor by her desire, that he might be introduced to her; she settled thirty pounds a year upon him, which was then no poor provision, made him one of the yeomen of the guards, and soon afterwards gave him the more fitting appointment of keeper of her select library at Richmond, called Merlin's Cave, where he had apartments assigned him, and was encouraged to pursue his studies so as to qualify himself for ordination in the Established Church. A volume of his verses was now published by subscription, and the names upon the list show with what zeal his friends had exerted themselves in the upper classes of society. Mr. Spence's account of the author was prefixed, and the volume was dedicated to the Queen, " as a humble tribute of duty, offered from a thankful heart to a gracious benefactress." He wrote a modest Preface, " to bespeak the reader's good nature, and to say something which might incline him to pardon what he could not commend. I have, indeed," said he, " but a poor defence to make for the things I have wrote: I do not think them good, and better judges will doubtless think worse of them than I do. Only this I may say of them, that if they have nothing to delight those who may chance to read them, they have nothing to give modesty a blush; if nothing to entertain and improve the mind, they have nothing to debauch and corrupt it. Another motive that I hope may induce the reader to overlook the defects in this volume is, that the oldest poem in it is little more than six years of age; and a considerable part of the time since that was writ, has been spent in endeavouring to learn a language of which I was then entirely ignorant."

He then apologized for his presumption in having attempted some translations from Horace, saying, that when only endeavouring to understand, he found it difficult to conquer the temptation of imitating some of the thoughts, which " mightily pleased" him. " I have not myself," he says, " been so fond of writing as might be imagined from seeing so many things of mine as are got together in this book. Several of these are on subjects which were given me by persons to whom I have such great obligations, that I always thought their desires commands. My want of education will be too evident from them for me to mention it here. And I hope when the reader weighs my performances, he will put *that* and other disadvantages into the scale. I would willingly here make known my obligations to those worthy persons who took notice of me in the midst of poverty and labour, were I not afraid my gratitude, thus publicly expressed, would offend them more than my silence. However, I must beg leave to return my thanks to a Reverend Gentleman of Wiltshire, and to another of Winchester: the former made my life more comfortable as soon as he knew me; the latter, after giving me several testimonies of his bounty and goodness, presented my first essays to a lady of quality attending the Queen, who made my low circumstances known to her Majesty. I hope, too, that all those honourable persons, whose names do me so much credit at the beginning of my book, will accept my acknowledgments and thanks for so liberal a subscription. And as this volume, I feel, will tell them they have not encouraged a poet, I will endeavour to let them see they have been generous to an honest man."

Swift, to his own discredit, wrote an ill-natured epigram upon him at this time:

" The thresher, Duck, could o'er the Queen prevail;
The proverb says, no fence against a flail.
From *threshing* corn, he turns to *thresh* his brains,
For which her Majesty allows him *grains;*
Tho' 'tis confest, that those who ever saw
His poems, think them all not worth *a straw*.
Thrice happy Duck, employed in threshing *stubble!*
Thy toil is lessen'd, and thy profits double."

The ill-will that called forth these lines was probably towards the Queen; and Swift cared not what pain the expression of it might give to the modest and meritorious man against whom it was directed. But Stephen had now obtained efficient patrons as well as steady friends; and he was in such reputation that Lord Palmerston appropriated the rent of an acre of land, for ever, to provide a dinner and strong beer for the threshers of Charlton at a public-house in that valley, in honour of their former comrade. The dinner is given on the 30th of June. The poet himself was present at one of these anniversaries, probably the first, and speaks thus of it in a pleasing poem addressed to that nobleman.

> " Oft as this day returns shall Threshers claim
> Some hours of rest, sacred to Temple's name;
> Oft as this day returns shall Temple cheer
> The Threshers' hearts with mutton, beef, and beer.
> Hence, when their children's children shall admire
> This holiday, and whence derived inquire,
> Some grateful father, partial to my fame,
> Shall thus describe from whence and how it came:—
> ' Here, child, a Thresher liv'd in ancient days;
> Quaint songs he sung and pleasing roundelays.
> A gracious Queen his sonnets did commend,
> And some great Lord, one Temple, was his friend.

That Lord was pleased this holiday to make,
And feast the Threshers for *that Thresher's* sake.'
Thus shall tradition keep my fame alive;
The bard may die—the Thresher still survive."

Having obtained orders, he was preferred to the living of Byfleet in Surrey. It has been said that this was " a singular and absurd transition, and that his small knowledge of Latin was surely not enough to justify such an abuse of church patronage." There can, however, be no doubt but that his attainments were such as fairly qualified him for this preferment; nor would Spence, (himself in all respects an exemplary and excellent man,) by whose influence he obtained it, have recommended him, had it been otherwise. His character, his inclination, and his abilities, were alike suited to this way of life; and he is said to have been much followed as a preacher, not only while novelty and his reputation were likely to attract congregations, but as long as he lived.

His end was an unhappy one; he became insane, threw himself into the water, near Reading, in 1756, and was drowned. Till that malady occurred he had been a useful parish priest, and approved himself every way worthy of the patronage which had been bestowed upon him. If the malady had shown itself earlier, it might have been ascribed to the transition from a life of great bodily labour to a sedentary one, and to excess in study; but as about thirty years had elapsed since he was taken from the barn, the cause is more likely to have been accidental, or constitutional. He had probably been always highly sensitive. Spence speaks of him as trembling when the scene betwen Hamlet and the Ghost was read to him. And he thus describes the effect produced upon him by the speeches of Antony over Cæsar's body: " as I was reading to him, I observed that his countenance changed often in the most moving parts. His eye was quick and busy all the time, and I never saw applause, or the shifting of proper passions appear so strongly in any face as in his." It was a fine, strongly-marked countenance, with regular features; but after his fate, the expression in his portrait which the artist intended for thoughtfulness or inspiration, might easily be interpreted as denoting melancholy, and a tendency to madness.

A catalogue of his books, as for sale, was published with those of two other persons soon after his decease. That they should have been numerous enough for this, implies that his love of reading had continued unabated, and that his circumstances had not been straitened. The kindness of his friends at court did not cease at his death, and his daughter was thus allowed to retain his apartments at Richmond.

Stephen Duck seems never to have entertained an overweening opinion of his own genius. Encouraged as he was, he would have written more if he had not been conscious that his talents for poetry were rather imitative than inventive; that he was incapable of imitating what he clearly saw was best; and that it was not likely he could produce any thing better than his first efforts. This is proof of his good sense. He was, indeed, a modest, diligent, studious, good man; and the patronage which he obtained is far more honourable to the spirit of his age, than the temper, which may censure or ridicule it, can be to ours.

Passing over the respectable name of Dodsley, because his poems and an account of his life are to be found in the General Collection of the British Poets, the next writer of the self-taught class is—

JAMES WOODHOUSE,

Of Rowley, near Hales-Oven, about seven miles from Birmingham, and two from the Leasowes. He was a village shoemaker, and though he had been taken from school at seven years old, had so far improved the little which he could possibly have learnt there, as to eke out his scanty means by teaching to read and write. He is first heard of at the age of three-and-twenty, and having then a wife and children. Shenstone had at that time found it necessary to forbid that general access to his grounds which he used to allow, so much mischief had wantonly been done there,—a disgraceful characteristic whereby the English populace are distinguished from those of any other country, and by which they injure themselves even more than they injure others, for they make it necessary to exclude them wherever they can be excluded. Woodhouse, upon this occasion, addressed some verses to him, entreating that he might be exempted from this prohibition, and permitted still to recreate himself and indulge his imagination in that sweet scenery; and Shenstone, who was always benevolent and generous, when he had inquired into the character of the petitioner, admitted him not only into his grounds, but to the use of his library also. His whole reading till then had been in magazines.

Shenstone found that the poor applicant used to work with a pen and ink at his side, while the last was in his lap;—the head at one employ, the hands at another; and when he had composed a couplet or a stanza, he wrote it on his knee. In one of the pieces thus composed, and entitled Spring, there are these affecting stanzas:—

> " But now domestic cares employ
>   And busy every sense,
> Nor leave one hour of grief or joy
>   But's furnish'd out from thence:
>
> Save what my little babes afford,
>   Whom I behold with glee,
> When smiling at my humble board,
>   Or prattling at my knee.
>
> Not that my Daphne's charms are flown,
>   These still new pleasures bring,
> 'Tis these inspire content alone;
>   'Tis all I've left of spring.

*   *   *   *

> I wish not, dear connubial state,
>   To break thy silken bands;
> I only blame relentless fate,
>   That every hour demands.
>
> Nor mourn I much my task austere,
>   Which endless wants impose;
> But oh! it wounds my soul to hear
>   My Daphne's melting woes!
>
> For oft she sighs and oft she weeps,
>   And hangs her pensive head,
> *While blood her furrowed finger steeps,*
>   *And stains the passing thread.*
>
> When orient hills the sun behold,
>   Our labours are begun:
> And when he streaks the west with gold,
>   The task is still undone."

These verses were pointed out to me, for their feeling and their truth, by the greatest poet of the age.

In 1764, five years after this poor man's fortunate introduction to Shenstone, a collection of his poems was published for his benefit, in quarto, price three shillings. It appears from a piece addressed to Shenstone, upon his "Rural Elegance," that the books to which he now had access, and the models to which his patron had directed his attention, had induced him to write in a more ambitious strain, and aim at some of the artifices of versification.

"What! cannot He, who form'd the fount of light,
 And shining orbs that ornament the night;
 Who hangs his silken curtains round the sky,
 And trims their skirts with fringe of every dye;
 In sheets of radiance spreads the solar beams
 With softened lustre o'er the tranquil streams;
 Or o'er the glittering surface softly flings
 The whispering winds with gently waving wings,
 While every kindled curl's resplendent rays
 Quick dart and drown in bright successive blaze;
 Who dipt in countless greens the lawns and bowers,
 And touch'd with every tint the faultless flowers;
 With beauty clothes each beast that roams the plain,
 And birds' rich plumes with ever-varied stain;
 Each fair-scaled fish in watery regions known,
 And insect's robe that mocks the coloured stone;
 Doth he not form the peasant's visual sphere
 To catch each charm that crowns the chequer'd year;
 Construct his ear to seize the passing sound,
 From wind, or wave, or wing, or whistle round;
 From breathing breeze, or tempest's aweful roar;
 Soft lisping rills, or Ocean's thundering shore;
 Unnumber'd notes that fill the echoing field,
 Or mingled minstrelsy the woodlands yield;
 The melting strains and melodies of song
 That float, impassioned, from the human tongue?

Or fondly feel each sound that sweetly slips
Thro' ear to heart, from favourite lover's lips;
And trace the nicer harmony that springs
From puny gnats' shrill-sounding treble wings;
Light fly's sharp counter; bee's strong tenor tone;
Huge hornet's bass, and beetle's drowsy drone;
Grasshopper's open shake, quick twittering all the day,
Or cricket's broken chirp, that chimes the night away?"

These lines are extracted, not from the original edition of his poems, but from a volume which he published after an interval of nearly forty years; it is not unlikely, therefore, that they may have been altered during that interval, and, in the author's opinion, improved by bringing them nearer to the fashion which was then in vogue. A process, indeed, is observable, both in the verses of Woodhouse and Stephen Duck, which might be looked for, as almost inevitable: they began by expressing their own thoughts and feelings, in their own language; all which, owing to their stations in life, had a certain charm of freshness as well as truth; but that attraction passes away when they begin to form their style upon some approved model, and they then produce just such verses as any person, with a metrical ear, may be taught to make by a receipt.

In this his second and last publication, the then forgotten author recalled attention to his name only by a modest motto: *Sutor ultra crepidam.* One passage may be selected, from many which show that he retained in an advanced age that love and enjoyment of natural beauties which were the means of obtaining for him Shenstone's friendly assistance.

> " Lovelier far than vernal flowers,
> The mushrooms shooting after showers;
> That fear no more the fatal scythe,
> But proudly spread their bonnets blythe,
> With coverings form'd of silk and snow,
> And lined with brightening pink below.
>
> * * * *
>
> But more the later fungus race,
> Begot by Phœbus' warm embrace
> In summer months on procreant earth,
> By damp September brought to birth;
> That, just like Jove, produce their seed
> From teeming brain for future breed.
> Their forms and hues some solace yield,
> In wood, or wild, or humid field,
> Whose tapering stems, robust or light,
> Like columns catch the searching sight,

To claim remark where'er I roam,
Supporting each a stately dome:
Like fair umbrellas furl'd or spread,
Display their many-colour'd head,
Grey, purple, yellow, white, or brown,
Shap'd like War's shield or Prelate's crown,
Like Freedom's cap, or Friar's cowl,
Or China's bright inverted bowl;
And while their broadening disks unfold
Gay silvery gills, or nets of gold,
Beneath their shady-curtain'd cove,
Perform all offices of love.
In beauty chief, the eye to chain,
'Mong whispering pines, or arid plain,
A glittering group assembled stands,
Like Elf's or Fay's embattled bands,
Where every arm appears to wield
With pigmy strength a giant shield,
And deeply dyed in sanguine gore,
With brazen bosses studded o'er;
While magic Fancy's ear confounds
The whistling winds with hostile sounds."

When this volume was published (1803) the author was living near Norbury Park, where he seems to have found a generous friend in Mr. Locke. He was then above sixty-eight years of age; I do not know when he died. In his case, as in Stephen Duck's, the persons who befriended him had the satisfaction of knowing that their kindness was well bestowed. And if the talents which they brought into notice were not of a kind in either case to produce, under cultivation, extraordinary fruits, in both a deserving man was raised from poverty, and placed in circumstances favourable to his moral and intellectual nature.

JOHN BENNET.

A few years after the publication of Woodhouse's first volume, another versifyer of the same calling appeared, whose name was John Bennet, and who worked as a journeyman shoemaker at Woodstock, where his father was parish clerk when Warton obtained the curacy of that town. Warton, who was remembered with affection by all who ever knew him, for his thorough good-nature, and the boyish hilarity which he retained through life, is said to have liked the father for his psalm-singing, and to have given the son some instruction for improving his rhymes. He seems to have rendered him greater service in assisting him to procure a very respectable list of subscribers.

There is nothing in his poems which deserves to be extracted for its own sake: a few lines, which express some of the popular prejudices concerning the alteration of the style, may serve as a fair specimen of their average merit, or rather demerit. An old man, conversing upon the subject on Christmas Eve, says—

— "He should ne'er with true devotion pray
Upon the morrow, call'd New Christmas Day.

Then tells of Glastonbury's holy thorn,
That buds and blossoms on the blessed morn;
Sets forth at large when pleasing midnight peal
On Christmas Eve the welcom'd season hail,
Before the altered time, the flocks and kine
At sound thereof felt impulse nigh divine;
And on their bended knees did straightway fall,
E'er since the era of the sacred stall.

" His dame then tells that her rosemary tree,
Until the old season is from blooming free,
But on that day is with new blossoms crown'd,
And sheds its fragrant odours all around.
Again the old man speaks his doubts and fears,
How since that time he was perplexed with cares;
'Cause in those days, so lost, 'twas plainly seen,
An holy sabbath day must intervene.
Then talks it o'er how dear all sorts of food
Did daily grow; nor can he hold it good,
But finds all things are worse since the altered time,
Therefore condemns it for a heinous crime."

Some things worthy of notice are incidentally mentioned in Bennet's verses: as that during a contested election for Oxfordshire, a zealous tallow-chandler made blue candles; and, that at Hampton-Gay, a village near the Cherwell, which he calls " great in yewy fame," there were the twelve apostles, flourishing in yew, Moses and Aaron, Susanna and the elders, all in evergreen likenesses; and moreover, a coach and horses, with coachman and footmen. Bennet relates, also, and with a proper feeling, that if a traveller arrived at Woodstock on a Sunday, during church time, and expressed an inclination to purchase gloves or cutlery, for both which that town was famous,—

——————— " Lo! messages are sent,
To those well skill'd, the precious wares to vent;
These, now at worship, clothed in ermined state,
And bending underneath the ponderous weight
Of magistracy, prayer and pomp resign,
To offer sacrifice at Mammon's shrine:
Yea, forthwith shun devotion as a crime,
Like Felix, leaving till another time."

ANN YEARSLEY.

Ann Yearsley's is a melancholy story. She was first heard of in 1784, when some verses were shown to Miss Hannah More as the production of a poor illiterate woman who sold milk from door to door. "The story," says Miss More, "did not engage my faith, but the verses excited my attention; for, though incorrect, they breathed the genuine spirit of poetry, and were rendered still more interesting by a certain natural and strong expression of misery, which seemed to fill the head and mind of the author. On making diligent inquiry into her history and character, I found that she had been born and bred in her present humble station, and had never received the least education, except that her brother had taught her to write. Her mother, who was also a milk-woman, appears to have had sense and piety, and to have given an early tincture of religion to this poor woman's mind. She is about eight-and-twenty, was married very young to a man who is said to be honest and sober, but of a turn of mind very different from her own. Repeated losses and a numerous family, for they had six children in seven years, reduced them very low; and the rigour of the last severe winter sunk them to the extremity of distress. Her aged mother, her six little infants, and herself (expecting every hour to lie in) were actually on the point of perishing, when the gentleman (Mr. Vaughan,) so gratefully mentioned in her poems, providentially heard of their distress, which I am afraid she had too carefully concealed, and hastened to their relief. The poor woman and her children were preserved; but for the unhappy mother all assistance came too late; she had the joy to see it arrive, but it was a joy she was no longer able to bear, and it was more fatal to her than famine had been." This " left a settled impression of sorrow on Mrs. Yearsley's mind."

" When I went to see her," Miss More continues, " I observed a perfect simplicity in her manners, without the least affectation or pretension of any kind, she neither attempted to raise my compassion by her distress, nor my admiration by her parts. But on a more familiar acquaintance, I have had reason to be surprised at the justness of her taste, the faculty I least expected to find in her. In truth, her remarks on the books she had read are so accurate, and so consonant to the opinions of the best critics, that from this very circumstance they would appear trite and commonplace to any one who had been in habits of society; for without having ever conversed with any body above her own level, she seems to possess the general principles of sound taste and just thinking." She had read Paradise Lost and the Night Thoughts, and was well acquainted with both; Pope's Eloisa, a few of Shakespeare's plays, and a translation of the Georgics, which seems particularly to have delighted her. Some classical allusions in her verses she had taken from prints in a shop window,..these gratuitous exhibitions, have, like bookstalls, contributed much to the delight and instruction of those upon whom the advantages of education would have been well bestowed. She had never seen a Dictionary, and knew nothing of grammatical rules. Her vocabulary therefore was that of the books which she had read, her syntax that of the ignorant and vulgar with whom she conversed. Miss More described her poems as like those of all unlettered poets, abounding in imagery, metaphor, and personification, her faults in that respect being rather those of superfluity than of want. "She thought her ear perfect, and the structure of her blank verse so happy and so varied, as even to appear skilful. You will find her," she says, " often diffuse from redundancy, and oftener obscure from brevity; but you will seldom find in her those inexplicable poetic sins, the false thought, the puerile conceit, the distorted image, and the incongruous metaphor, the common resources of bad poets, and the not uncommon blemishes of good ones."

A small volume of her Poems was now published by subscription, the grosser inaccuracies of language having been corrected. Miss More was a most efficient as well as kind patroness; and the volume in consequence went through a second and a third edition. " It is not intended," said that patroness, " to place her in such a state of independence as might seduce her to devote her time to the idleness of poetry. I hope she is convinced that the making of verses is not the great business of human life; and that as a wife and a mother she has duties to fill, the smallest of which is of more value than the finest verses she can write. But as it has pleased God to give her these talents, may they not be made as instruments to mend her situation? Pressing as her distresses are, if I did not think her heart was rightly turned I should be afraid of proposing such a measure, lest it should unsettle the sobriety of her mind, and, by exciting her vanity, indispose her for the laborious employments of her humble condition; but it would be cruel to imagine that we cannot mend her fortune without impairing her virtue. For my own part I do not feel myself actuated by the idle vanity of a *discoverer;* for I confess that the ambition of bringing to light a genius buried in obscurity, operates much less powerfully on my mind than the wish to rescue a meritorious woman from misery; for it is not fame, but bread, which I am anxious to secure to her."

The sum of 350*l.* arising from the first edition of these poems, and the presents made by some of the subscribers, was placed in the funds in the names of Mrs. Montague and Miss Hannah More, as trustees, for the benefit of Mrs. Yearsley and her children. This occasioned an unfortunate difference between the authoress and her first benefactress. Mrs. Yearsley wished to be admitted as a joint-trustee, and that the money should be equally divided according to the number of her children, and subject to their demand as each arrived at the age of twenty-one. The latter part of the proposal was improvident, the former seemed to imply a caution which, because it was felt to be unnecessary, was thought to be ungrateful. Some angry altercation ensued, and the acrimonious feelings thus excited were not soothed by the interference of friends on Mrs. Yearsley's behalf. It ended in a resignation of the trust, and in a lasting breach between the parties. The whole transaction was vexatious to Miss More, whose benevolent intentions ought not to have been misunderstood; and it was unfortunate for Mrs. Yearsley, who was now represented as a thankless and unworthy person, and who from that time considered as an enemy one who, but for this misunderstanding, would have continued to be her friend and faithful adviser.

Mrs. Yearsley prefixed a narrative in vindication of herself to the fourth edition of her Poems in 1786, and in the following year published a second collection by subscription. She now opened a Circulating Library at Bristol Hot Wells, but not upon a scale which could prove attractive, nor was the place one where much support was to be expected. In 1791 she produced a tragedy called Earl Goodwin, which was represented with little success at the Bristol and Bath Theatres. And in 1795 she published the Royal Captives, an unfinished novel, founded upon the mysterious story of the Iron Mask. "One of my motives," she says, "for publishing the work unfinished is, that the world may speak of me as I am, while I have power to hear. The clouds that hang over my fortunes intervene between me and the public; I incessantly struggle to dissipate them, and feel those struggles vain, and shall drop in the effort. This consolation I shall however bear with me to the verge of life, that to those who have guided me by the sacred and lambent flame of friendship, my memory will be dear."

This book was noticed in the Monthly Review, with a better feeling than is usually found in periodical criticisms. The unknown writer remarked the striking contrast between the strength of thought and the weakness of judgement which were apparent in the composition, "the almost continued inflation of the style, and the frequent power of expression, the crude and disjointed manner in which the story was planned and pursued, and the occasional force discovered in the incidents, the characters, and the philosophy at which the authoress aimed. The incidents are generally improbable, not because events more strange and incredible have not happened, but because in the writer's haste to produce great events she has neglected the minutiæ which are necessary for that purpose. From the same mistake there is a want of progression in the story. Having related one striking incident which she has not possessed patience and judgement enough to prepare, she hurries forward to another, and thus robs each of that force which she has been so ardent to impart.—If the reader of these volumes has thought before, they will lead him to think again. Those who buy books will much more frequently buy worse than better; and those who love to encourage an enterprizing and, however abashed and subdued, no vulgar spirit, will not think their money ill bestowed."

Mrs. Yearsley published one or two occasional poems before this, her last publication. The culture which she received, such as it was, came too late; nor does she appear to have derived any other advantage from it than that it enabled her to write with common grammatical accuracy. With extraordinary talents, strong feelings, and an ardent mind, she never produced a poem which found its way into any popular collection; and very few passages can be extracted from her writings which would have any other value than as indicating powers which the possessor knew not how to employ. But it ought to be observed here, that I have never seen either her novel or her tragedy. The best lines which I have noticed are in her second publication.

" ——————————— Cruel the hand
Which tears the veil of time from black dishonour;
Or, *with the iron pen of Justice, cuts*
Her cypher on the scars of early shame."

There is a like felicity of expression in these lines on the remembrance of her mother:—

" How oft with thee, when life's keen tempest howl'd
Around our heads, did I contented sit,
Drinking the wiser accents of thy tongue,
Listless of threatening ill. *My tender eye*
Was fix'd on thine, inquisitively sad.
Whilst thine was dim with sorrow: yet thy soul
Betray'd no innate weakness, but resolv'd
To tread thy sojourn calm and undismay'd."

Flourishing reputations (of the gourd tribe) have been made by writers of much less feeling and less capability than are evident in these lines. Ann Yearsley, though gifted with voice, had no strain of her own whereby to be remembered, but she was no mocking-bird.

She died at Melksham in 1806. Her affairs had not been prosperous, and it has been said that she was deranged for some time before her death. I know not what foundation there may have been for this report, more than the probability that such an effect would be wrought upon a highly sensitive mind by embarrassments, disappointments, the sense of supposed injuries, and the perpetual consciousness that her powers, not having been kindlily developed, had failed to produce, what, under favourable circumstances, they could not have failed to bring forth.

The temporary success of Mrs. Yearsley contributed to bring into notice another illiterate versifyer of the same city: this was

JOHN FREDERICK BRYANT,

Who was born in Market Street, St. James's, Westminster, 1753. His father was a native of Bristol, and had been bred a tobacco-pipe-maker, the grandfather and all his family being of that business. Not liking the trade he removed to London, worked as a journeyman house painter, and married a servant maid, whose parents were poor honest hard-working people at Sunbury. When Bryant was about fourteen months old he was taken by these relations, who intended to keep him only while his mother was confined with a second infant; but they grew fond of the child, and he remained with them till he was five years old. He was then removed to London, and after a twelvemonths stay was again taken back to Sunbury in a very ill state of health, which he himself always believed was occasioned by grief at his separation from the old people, who were remarkably fond of him, and whose affection had produced in him a corresponding love. " My mother," he says, " had at that time, besides me, my two sisters to look after,..one of them quite an infant; and as she also worked very hard at washing and ironing, it consequently did not lie in her way to give me a great deal of indulgence; but my grandmother unjustly suspected her of using me ill." There he recovered and remained till the year 1760, when his father, accepting a proposal to settle at Bristol, and there follow his original calling, removed thither with his family, and took with him this his eldest child. The boy was greatly affected at being a second time " torn from the worthy old people and his beloved Sunbury." He lost his health again, and it was but slowly that his constitution recovered from the effects of the change. He was put to school to an old woman, who taught him to read, and a year of such schooling was all that fell to his lot; for he was then kept at home and employed in packing up tobacco pipes for exportation. " I had now at intervals," he says, " a great deal of leisure; yet though in the country I had been very fond of play, I retained but little inclination for it at this time. Indeed I was but ill fit to be in company with other boys; for I was grown very deaf, and had besides acquired a kind of timidity and bashfulness, which together made me appear very foolish, and occasioned many people to set me down as little better than an idiot."

The lessons at school had given him no love of reading. The first thing which he read with pleasure was the History of Joseph and his brethren, in an abridgment of the Book of Genesis, which his mother gave him. Other abridgments of the Scriptures delighted him so much, that at length he read the whole Bible; and could not, he says, help lamenting that he should have been " born in an age in which prophets, prodigies, and miracles, with the frequent visibility of God and angels, were not to be seen or expected." He acquired also at this time what he calls an immoderate fondness for the wonderful, " preferring by far the stories of giants, fairies, magicians, or heroes performing impossibilities, to any history or narrative that wore the face of truth." Some books of this description, the last of the blackletter race, " were part of the lumber of a set of dusty shelves" in his father's house. The only one which Bryant mentions is the Destruction of Troy, under which title old Caxton's work (the first book printed in the English language,) slightly modernized, so long ago that the very modernizations have an antiquated cast, entertained his boyhood, as some four-and-twenty years later it did mine. His father bought for him that account of the Heathen Gods, from which magazine poets in former days derived their stock of classical knowledge; there he found quotations from Pope's Homer and Dryden's Virgil, which so pleased his ear and delighted his imagination, that he read them again and again, till he had most of them by heart. And at ten years old, when he was learning to write, he tried to make verses. "I remember," he says, "my mother's once laughing heartily upon finding an Invocation to the Muses, in one of my little attempts, the sublime and interesting subject of which was—the description and character of our turnspit-dog. However, my father seemed to be pleased with my humour for rhyming, and would often read my fragments to his acquaintances. I was also very fond of pictures, particularly of landscapes, which I took great pleasure in attempting to draw, as by taking notice of the diminution of distant, and the foreshortening of oblique objects, in those lively representations of nature, I had obtained a little notion of perspective. Many of my rude productions in this line likewise were, by the partiality of a father, supposed not totally destitute of merit, and were by him often shown as curiosities."

He had another source of enjoyment in music, which he enjoyed the more, because, on the restoration of his hearing, it came to him like the developement of a new sense. And he had opportunities of enjoying it, for the father had some skill in music, was sometimes employed to play at the Assembly Room, and was acquainted with most of the Bath and Bristol musicians, who sometimes had their rehearsals at his house. Seeing the boy's inclination he thought of giving him some instructions, but ill days came on, which left him no time for any thing but hard and hopeless labour. Among the numerous families which the American war reduced to poverty and want, was that of this poor pipe-maker. Till the troubles which broke out about the Stamp Act commenced, his business had been a good one, and though he had a large family he was in tolerable circumstances, having sufficient for the day and no cause to be anxious for the morrow. He had then employed ten journey-people; the loss of his export trade compelled him to part with them all, and depend upon the labour of his own family, though out of nine children there were but four whose services could be of any use, and his profits soon became inadequate to support them. A trifling salary as one of the city trumpeters, and the office of Exchange Keeper, which the Corporation afterwards gave him, and which added to his means ten pounds a year, enabled him to go on, but with difficulty; and it now became matter of complaint against poor Bryant, that he attended too much to his books and too little to his work. The occupation was one which he greatly disliked, for it had been his wish to go to sea: he acknowledges that he neglected his business, and that his parents had cause to be displeased with him on that score. At length they forbade him to read, except on Sundays. "But my mind," he says, "was ever among books. Natural philosophy, and particularly astronomy, began at this time to be the favourite subject of my contemplation; but while my mind was busy, endeavouring to explain the mechanism of terrestrial nature, or soaring among the stars, the labour of my hands turned out to little amount; the less so, as I was extraordinarily slow and awkward at my work, even when I did my best and set my mind most upon it, which I believe was owing to the very great dislike I ever had to the business."

Sunday was now to him more than a day of rest; it was a day of recreation also; he was generally invited to dine and sup with a blind acquaintance of his father's, who was amused by hearing him read, procured books for that purpose, and generally gave him twopence for this innocent Sabbath day's work. This money was all that he possessed, and he commonly laid it out in prints and colours, with which he amused himself by stealth. He was now above eighteen; and longing once more to see his poor old grand-parents, who had loved him so tenderly in his childhood, seeing no chance of ever obtaining leave to visit them, and fearing that death would soon put it finally out of his power, he determined to do so without asking his father's consent. Accordingly he wrote the first letter that he ever penned, informing them of his purpose, desired that they would not acquaint his mother with it, but in their next letter mention something by which he might know they had received his, as he had no friend whom he could trust to receive a letter for him. The poor old people wrote presently according to his wish, and in the month of October he set off with a little bundle of clothes, two or three books, and three-halfpence, being the whole of his worldly wealth.

In another respect Bryant was ill prepared for this pilgrim's progress, which a feeling of natural piety had made him undertake. Having lived in the heart of a great city, and been kept at work in it during six days of the week, he had never in his life walked ten miles at a stretch; and having more than doubled that distance when on the first day's journey he reached Chippenham, he found that he was a very bad traveller. There he sold his Bible for sixpence. The next day (being Sunday) he reached Marlborough, through a heavy rain; and was then rendered so ill by the unusual exertion, that he found it necessary to remain there all Monday, selling his best hat for eighteen pence. On Tuesday evening he got to Thatcham, and paid his last twopence for a night's lodging. The next day he walked from morning till night without any other refreshment than a little water, reached Twyford, and sold another book for sixpence. Another day brought him to Brentford, and there he pawned an article of his apparel for sixpence. Friday he entered London, found out some acquaintance of his mother, and learned from them that he might have reached Sunbury without coming to the metropolis. But he was now better able to walk, he was in good spirits also at being so near his resting place; his friends supplied him with some refreshment and a little money, and he reached the place of his destination that same night, where the good old people received him "with the most immoderate joy." Next day his grandmother made him write home in her name, desiring his parents to forgive the step which he had taken on their account, as they should not have died in peace if they had not seen him.

He staid with them nine days, which were nine of the happiest he had ever seen, and then departed with the greatest regret, promising to visit them again during the next summer. A little money was raised for his journey; he walked back much better than he had done when outward bound, and got home in health and spirits after an absence of three weeks. His father received him kindly; but "I leave any one of common feeling," he says, " to judge with what astonishment and horror I heard him, when he abruptly informed me that my poor mother (who was big with child) was dead and buried. The letter which I wrote she never saw, as it was not delivered till about two hours after she had expired. We were all in the greatest affliction, as we had reason to be, on the death of so good a mother; but my grief was beyond measure increased by the unfortunate circumstance of my being in such a manner absent from home at the melancholy crisis, the more so as many people laid her death entirely to that account."

The loss of an excellent wife left upon Bryant's father a lasting melancholy; increasing difficulties tended to sour his temper, and he had some cause for being displeased with his son, who confesses that all the strength of repeated resolutions could not make him confine his attachment to his business, so that in the performance of his work he generally fell short even of what, unskilful as he was, he ought to have done. Though conscious of this, he thought himself unkindly treated, and finding himself altogether unhappy in his father's house, he left it a second time about sixteen months after his return, " with as little ceremony as at first." The old people at Sunbury who had so dearly loved him were both dead. His intention was to go to sea, where he thought his sober disposition might help him to preferment: and he meant at the end of each voyage to employ his wages, as far as they would go, in acquiring some knowledge of mathematics. It would have been useless he thought to look for a ship in Bristol, his father being so well known there, and so much respected, that no merchant or master of a vessel would have willingly received him without his consent. He went to London therefore; but it was at a time when able seamen could hardly obtain employment, so he was glad to get work at his own business. This soon failed, and he then led a precarious life, sometimes in his old employ, then as a labourer at Woolwich, where they were digging foundations for the barracks; there he was disabled by the ground falling in upon him, and consequently discharged. He then got into work sometimes with a tobacco-pipe-maker at Woolwich, who was a Bristol man, sometimes as a jobber in the rope-grounds, and when both occupations failed, he attended on the quays, and now and then got a job at the cranes; but there were at that time so many men of all descriptions out of employ, that if there was a job for four or five men to perform, there were generally twenty to scramble for it; and not being so good a scrambler as many of his competitors, he could not earn a bare subsistence, so that he was obliged to part with every thing he could possibly spare, and was once so hard put to it as to go without a morsel of food from Saturday afternoon till Monday night.

At this time he would have enlisted as a soldier in the East India service, if it had not been for a remaining sense of duty to his father, who had always declared his utter disapprobation of any such step. His health began greatly to fail; but he again obtained employment with the pipe-maker, though it hardly enabled him to subsist. Having sent some account of his distress to his father, he was directed to some one in reply, who gave him a few shillings, with an injunction to return to Bristol. He promised and intended to do so, but could not, he says, bear the thoughts of going back in such a state and garb as he was then in. He was now employed for nearly two years at the barracks and other public works, carrying a hod for the bricklayers, under which hard labour it pleased God, he says, to give him an amazing increase of strength, so that after a little use he performed it with surprising alacrity. This improvement in his health and wages enabled him to send some trifling presents to his brother and sisters, and at the same time he told his father that if it was then his pleasure he would return immediately. The answer was that his father had been two months dead; that his sister with a brother's help carried on the little business left, which was barely sufficient to maintain those who were in it, and that most of the younger children were in a fair way of being provided for in the public schools. So he was desired not to return.

Meantime, while a laborious life had strengthened a weak constitution, a precarious one, with its full share of privation and distress, had neither broken a strong spirit, nor damped a cheerful one. His talent of stringing together rhymes made him a favourite with most of his comrades, and held others in some degree of awe,..he had commenced a satire upon one of them in consequence of a dispute, and the fear of being thus berhymed so worked upon the offender, that he stopt the satirist's progress by giving a treat of beef-steaks and porter. An opportunity offered of entering upon his own business on his own account, if he could raise a little money in part of payment for the tools and fixtures of the shop from which his friend the Bristol-man was removing. Some of the foremen under whom he had worked readily lent him a few pounds; but when that difficulty was removed, an old grievance stood in his way.

The Bristol-man sometime before had asked him to lampoon the daughter of the person to whom the house and shop belonged. He had done this in no measured terms, and was now properly rewarded for it, for the landlord refused to let him the shop, and the expense of removing the fixtures and erecting a new kiln would have been more than he could venture to engage in. Thus disappointed sorely, and probably little pleased with himself for having given the provocation which brought the disappointment on, he resolved upon going to sea, and entered accordingly on board a privateer.

When he had been a fortnight on board, the captain learnt that he was near-sighted, and discharged him for that defect, paying him for the time he had been on board. Poor Bryant had no sooner been set ashore at Wapping than he found that the character of a seaman is by the law—or custom—of England indelible. He was seized by a press-gang, and dreading the treatment on board a man of war, thought himself fortunate when the landlady of their rendezvous interceded for him, and the alternative was offered him of entering the gang. "That choice," he says, "was soon made, and my hand with horror embraced the lawless bludgeon. But here I was in one thing agreeably surprised: I had looked on all in this employment as persons of the most abandoned principles; but I found those with whom I served to be men of great civility and real good nature; and I must do them the justice to affirm, that for the time I was with them I never saw an instance of unnecessary cruelty or insult. We were commanded by Lieutenant Chubb, of the Princess Royal, a gentleman of the greatest humanity. But I was certainly in a very disagreeable situation, being witness to a variety of distress, which could not otherwise than be the effect of our operations, though conducted with the greatest tenderness." It was not long before the landlady obtained his discharge; there was little difficulty in doing this as he was no seaman; and she took him into her service during the illness of a person who looked after her business. While he was thus employed he wrote a song, not ill adapted for the purpose, inviting men to enter on board the lieutenant's ship.

As his acquaintance with the press-gang and their officer must have led him to look with less dislike upon the naval service, he might probably have entered therein, if he had not about this time formed an attachment to a young woman, which led to an engagement between them. The effect was what such engagements usually produce upon those whose principles are good: it put an end to his precarious course of life. He went to Bristol, hoping to settle there in his own trade, and fixed a time when he was to return to London to be married, and bring back his wife. When that time came the press was hot, and it would have been dangerous for him to have travelled; he proposed therefore that his betrothed should come to him; and when they met and weighed all circumstances, she thought it would be imprudent to venture upon marrying till his circumstances were better, and that the best plan was for her to get into service at Bristol, and there wait for better times. This was too reasonable for Bryant to gainsay it, for he had hitherto made no progress toward setting up on his own account, but had worked with his brother and sister, their little profit serving for their common maintenance. He now took to a void workshop on their premises, made use of some old tools and fixtures of his father's which were lying unused, and began making pipes for himself, the same kiln serving both him and his sister. Some years past with little success on his part, but there was something to look on to which sweetened life, and his was a hopeful and a cheerful spirit.

He had begun his first attempt in verse by duly invoking the Muse, for, as he had read in the Pantheon, " let no person despise the Muses unless he designs to bring destruction upon himself." It was his good hap, contrary to general experience, to find that theirs is no thankless service; and his first proof of this was that by making songs for some convivial meetings which he frequented, and singing them himself, he procured friends and customers, and occasioned moreover a consumption of his own tobacco-pipes. Fortune seeming then a little to relent, and his affairs beginning to wear rather a more favourable aspect, he married. As this had not been done in haste, it was not repented at leisure. His wife worked very hard in the business, and attended his customers in the city, while he went about the country with a hamper of pipes upon his shoulders, travelling in this manner ten, fifteen, and often twenty miles out. This he generally did twice a week; and sometimes amused himself during these solitary excursions by composing verses as he trudged along. One of those afflictions against which no prudence can provide threw him back in the world. "My wife," he says, "lying-in, we bore the expense tolerably. To be sure our profit had not turned out so much as we could have earned at journey-work; still the hopes of getting into more business kept up our spirits. But my wife catching cold rather before her month was expired, it unfortunately affected one of her breasts in such a manner, that after every other experiment had been tried, she was forced to submit to the operation of the surgeon's knife; and was on the whole near half-a-year under his hands, during which time she was incapable of affording me any assistance."

Soon after her recovery he was informed that there was a house lying void at Swansea, in which tobacco-pipes had been formerly manufactured, and where all the fixtures, tools, &c. were remaining since the death of the late occupier. Bryant thought it worth while to set out for that place, in hope of taking the house (as he knew it to be a place of considerable trade), or if that failed, of getting a few orders; so he departed on a Saturday afternoon, taking with him a few shillings-worth of his goods by the sale of which to bear his expenses. This little cargo he was lucky enough to dispose of before he reached the New Passage. " Arriving there a good while before bed time, I sat in the kitchen of the inn," he says, " contemplating my schemes, and enjoying by anticipation the advantages I should probably derive by having the monopoly of a capital sea-port town, till from this pleasing reverie I was awakened by a farmer attempting to sing, which, through intoxication, finding himself incapable of doing, after several efforts, he gave it over, to the regret of some of the company who had asked him for a song. Upon which, from a natural desire to please, I seized the opportunity to offer them one myself; which being accepted and sung, so well pleased them, that from one song to another, they kept me at it till almost midnight; in the mean time I partook of the good cheer of the company scot-free."

Trifling as this incident seemed at the time, it speedily in its consequences turned the tide of his fortune. Arriving at Swansea after two days delightful walk, on the Monday, he found that the house for which he came to treat had been for more than a twelvemonth occupied, and by one in a different branch of business. Thus ended his hopes; the next day he obtained orders for as large a quantity of pipes as he could get ready within a certain time, set off on his return towards evening, and slept at Neath. On the following morning his stock of money was reduced to a few halfpence, which in the course of the day was so far reduced by other calls, that there did not remain enough to pay for a night's lodging, and after walking till night had closed, he took shelter in a barn near Cardiff. His condition had never been more forlorn, for he had not enough to pay for his fare across the Severn; however he trudged on, trusting to Providence, which had better things in store for him than he had dreamt of, even in his warmest hopes, and reached the Passage House between three and four on the following afternoon, some three hours before the tide served for crossing. The good nature and the social talents, of which he had given proof there a few nights before, were remembered by some of the boatmen who had been then his boon companions; they recognised him at the door, shook hands with him heartily, and insisted on his favouring them with a few songs while they waited for the tide. Bryant told them in reply, that he had travelled so far with an empty pocket and an empty stomach as to be incapable of singing, and he informed them of his additional distress in not having wherewithal to pay his passage. The good-natured fellows soon set both his stomach and his heart at rest; they promised him that he should not be left behind, called for bread and cheese, and regaled him with drink. So being thus put in tune he sung several songs, and the kitchen rung once more with his voice and the applause of his delighted auditors.

At this time a gentleman arrived, and being too much in haste to wait for the passage-boat, ordered the small one to be got ready. While this was doing and the stranger was taking some refreshment, Bryant contined to amuse the company in the kitchen. He was standing at the door when the gentleman went down to the beach, and perceiving that the person who attended him could not conveniently carry the luggage to the water side, he lent a hand. The gentleman then asked if he was going to pass; offered him a seat in the boat, and said, " you shall sing me one or two of your songs on the way, and when we get on the other side I will give you something to wet your whistle." When they were fairly under sail Bryant began, and having ended the song, asked leave to sing one of his own making, for he was a poet himself. This he said, expecting only to occasion a laugh. But the gentleman listened attentively, made him repeat other of his verses, pointed out some mis-pronunciations, and drew from him the particulars of his situation. When they were on shore he made Bryant a present, gave him his address, desired him to send him copies of one or two of the pieces which he particularly admired, and told him he might expect to hear from him ere long.

Bryant has not mentioned the name of his benefactor, nor left any clue by which it might be discovered; that stranger, therefore, must have been one of those who like not to have their good deeds known. A most effectual benefactor he proved; he moved in high life, and introduced Bryant to so many persons who liked to do good, and were wealthy enough to gratify their bountiful inclinations, that the poor rhymer was enabled by their liberality to give up a miserable occupation, in which his eyes suffered from exposure to the fire, and to set up as a stationer, bookbinder, and printseller in London. There, in 1787, he published a collection of his verses, chiefly for the purpose of presenting it to those who had assisted in relieving him from a state of extreme indigence. A brief advertisement was prefixed by some friendly and judicious person, saying, that it had been thought respectful by some of his encouragers, to prefix a few lines concerning the author and the verses which were now made public. He had been found, upon the fullest inquiry, to be a man of strict probity, and to have supported the character of an industrious and honest man when struggling with a degree of poverty more than sufficient to have repressed the indulging of a poetical inclination. The verses were intended for the perusal of those who might be desirous of seeing the gradual progress of natural poetical genius, unassisted by education, and therefore it had been thought proper to print progressive specimens of them, from the first essay down to the work on which he was at that time engaged. Peculiar merit was not to be looked for in the earlier poems, separately considered; but such readers as might find no amusement in observing the growth of a poetical spirit, might possibly find their time not misspent in reading some of the later compositions. A long list of benefactors followed the advertisement; and an account of his life, written by himself, and exactly as he wrote it, except as to the spelling, was prefixed to the verses.

From this small collection, for it fills only four

octavo sheets, a few specimens will exemplify the writer's capabilities. The first is from one of his convivial pieces.

> "Now some folks like your hunting song,
>   Some sing about the wars,
> For some men of the chase are fond,
>   And a few of the field of Mars.
> While some affect your toping songs,
>   (The votaries of wine,)
> The lover swears your love-sick songs
>   Are the only songs divine.
>
> The sailor likes your sea-songs best,
>   In which he'll take some pride,
> And wonder if he lets you rest
>   Till he has sung you a full broadside.
> The miller sings his mill-clack song;
>   Your party songs for some;
> The husbandman holds fast the can,
>   Loud roaring harvest home?"

The theme then changes, and he proceeds to extol the glories of a convivial meeting at the Sun in Christmas Street. Reader, I am a Bristol-man myself by birth, and remember the sign; and remember poor Bryant's workshop in the same street, which for several years I passed morning and evening, with a satchel in my hand, or across my shoulder, on my way to and from school. I remember the shop at the distance of five-and-forty years, by its wretched appearance; and Bryant himself I must often have seen there, smeared with pipe-clay, and his eyes bleared by the furnace. Even then, however, these lines will show that there were hours when he was "o'er all the ills of life victorious," though he did not pursue his victory so far as Tam o'Shanter.

> "Our lips the circling tankard greeting,
>   Our pipes with fragrance charge the air;
> Success we drink, and every draught repeating,
>   Or damn the churl, or toast the fair.
>
> While thus the social joys are flowing,
>   In every eye while pleasures beam,
> While with celestial flame each breast is glowing,
>   The sky-born sons of Jove we seem.
>
> Meanwhile the song in strains harmonious,
>   With Fancy's flights enchants our ears,
> Now hear the thundering chorus roar symphonious,
>   And stun the world and drown the spheres,—
>   And stun the world and drown the spheres."

In a very different strain are these lines, addressed to a piece of unwrought pipe-clay; the author probably intended them for a sonnet, a species of poem for which at that time he was not likely to have had any other models than Milton and Charlotte Smith.

"Rude mass of earth, from which with moiled hands
    (Compulsive taught) the brittle tubes I form,
    Oft listless, while my vagrant fancy warm
Roves, heedless of necessity's demands,
Amid Parnassian bowers, or wishful eyes
    The flight of genius, while sublime she soars,
    Of moral truth in search, or earth explores,
Or sails with science through the starry skies:
Yet must I own, unsightly clod! thy claim
    To my attention, for thou art my stead.
    When grows importunate the voice of need,
    And in the furnace thy last change I speed,
Ah! then how eager do I urge the flame,
How anxious watch thee, 'mid that glowing fire
That threats my eye-balls with extinction dire."

The last specimen which I shall produce is a prayer: it is the best of his productions.

"Amid the ceaseless din of human strife,
    The groans of entering and departing life;
    Amid the songs of joy, the wails of woe,
    That living nature utters here below;

Amid the harmony of all the spheres:
In concert, unenjoy'd by mortal ears;
Amid Heaven's trumpets loud, by angels blown,
And lyres of seraphim, around thy throne,
O great Supreme! and while their voices join,
Proclaiming praise and glory only thine,
Presuming more, perhaps, than angels dare,
A trembling worm of earth intrudes his prayer.

  Thou great, eternal, awful, gracious cause
Of Nature's being, motion, form, and laws!
That gav'st me tastes of pleasure and of pain;
That gav'st me passions, which alternate reign,
And reason, passion's riot to restrain:
By whom I first inspir'd this mortal breath;
In whom I trust for being after death;
Should I enjoy thy first great blessing, health;
And should thy providence bestow me wealth,
And crown me parent of a numerous race,
Whose virtues should my name and fortune grace;
To love, to duty should my fair adhere;
Should ev'ry friend approve himself sincere;
Shouldst Thou my life reserve to ripest age,
And give me all the wisdom of the sage;
O! let no cursed avarice my store
Withhold from friend distress'd, or from the poor!
In love, or friendship, or paternal care,
In each enjoyment with the world I share,
Through life, O! give this feeling heart to be,
For ever warm with gratitude to Thee!

But should thy wisdom the reverse ordain,
And send me pale disease, and life-consuming pain;
Should pinching poverty still keep me down,
To pine beneath my fellow-mortals' frown;
Did I paternal feelings never know,
Or should my fruitful loins bring future woe;
Should an unfaithful wife dishonour bring;
Should slight of fancied friends my bosom wring;
Should my weak mind endure the scoff of fame,
And Dulness be my substituted name;
Should nature early find herself outworn,
And that her earth to earth must soon return,
Without a friend to comfort or to mourn—
Amidst this gloomy complicated throng
Of sharp afflictions, while I press along,
Through each, or real pain or seeming ill,
O give me resignation to thy will!

From a pencil note in Mr. Park's copy of Bryant's verses, I learn that he was patronized by the Chief Baron Macdonald...that he removed from Long Acre to the Strand...which seems to imply that he was prosperous in his new trade... and that he died there of consumption in 1791.

I do not introduce Robert Bloomfield here, because his poems are worthy of preservation separately, and in general collections; and because it is my intention one day to manifest at more length my respect for one whose talents were of no common standard, and whose character was in all respects exemplary. It is little to the credit of the age, that the latter days of a man whose name was at one time so deservedly popular, should have been past in poverty, and perhaps shortened by distress, that distress having been brought on by no misconduct or imprudence of his own.

A newspaper paragraph, which has been inserted in one of the volumes before me, quotes from Sheridan the elder, an illnatured passage in allusion to the writers who have here been noticed. " Wonder," he says, " usually accompanied by a bad taste, looks only for what is uncommon; and if a work comes out under the name of a thresher, a bricklayer, a milkwoman, or—a lord, it is sure to be eagerly sought after by the million."

" Persons of quality" require no defence when they appear as authors in these days: and, indeed, as mean a spirit may be shown in traducing a book because it is written by a lord, as in extolling it beyond its deserts for the same reason. But when we are told that the thresher, the milkwoman, and the tobacco-pipe-maker did not deserve the patronage they found,—when it is laid down as a maxim of philosophical criticism that poetry ought never to be encouraged unless it is **excellent in its kind**,—that it is an art in which inferior execution is not to be tolerated,—a luxury, and must therefore be rejected unless it is of the very best,—such reasoning may be addressed with success to cockered and sickly intellects, but it will never impose upon a healthy understanding, a generous spirit, or a good heart.

Bad poetry—(if it be harmless in its intent and tendency)—can do no harm, unless it passes for good, becomes fashionable, and so tends to deprave still further a vitiated public taste, and still further to debase a corrupted language. Bad criticism is a much worse thing, because a much more injurious one, both to the self-satisfied writer and the assentient reader; not to mention that without the assistance of bad criticism, bad poetry would but seldom make its way.

The mediocres have long been a numerous and an increasing race, and they must necessarily multiply with the progress of civilization. But it would be difficult to say wherefore it should be treated as an offence against the public, to publish verses which no one is obliged either to purchase or to read. Booksellers are not likely to speculate at their own cost in such wares; there is a direct gain to other branches of trade; employment is given where it is wanted; and if pecuniary loss be a matter of indifference to the author, there is then no injury to himself, and he could not have indulged himself in a more innocent folly, if folly it should deserve to be called. But if he is a good and amiable man, he will be both the better and the happier for writing verses. " Poetry," says Landor, " opens many sources of tenderness, that lie for ever in the rock without it."

If, indeed, a poet feels in himself a constant craving for reputation, and a desire of depreciating those who have been more successful than himself,—if he looks upon them as his competitors and rivals, not as his brethren in the art,—then verily it is unfortunate for such a man that he possesses the talent of versifying. And in that case he will soon betake himself to criticism, as a more congenial calling; for bad poets become malevolent critics, just as weak wine turns to vinegar.

The benevolent persons who patronized Stephen Duck, did it, not with the hope of rearing a great poet, but for the sake of placing a worthy man in a station more suited to his intellectual endowments, than that in which he was born. Bryant was befriended in a manner not dissimilar, for the same reason. In the cases of Woodhouse and Ann Yearsley, the intention was to better their condition in their own way of life. The Woodstock shoemaker was chiefly indebted for the patronage which he received, to Thomas Warton's good-nature, for my predecessor Warton was the best natured man that ever wore a great wig. My motives for bringing forward the present attempts in verse have already been explained.

It will be seen, from Mr. Jones's account of himself, that his opportunities of self-instruction have been even less than were possessed by any of the uneducated aspirants who preceded him. Had it been his fortune to have enjoyed those advantages, of which the great majority of educated persons make no use whatever after they become their own masters, he might in all probability have held more than a respectable place among the poets of his age; and the whole tenor of his conduct shows that he would have done his duty in any station of life to which he might have been called. But except during the time when he had access

CONCLUSION. 167

to Shakespeare's plays, he seems to have read little other poetry than what is occasionally to be found in provincial newspapers. From them he has sometimes copied a pattern, or a tune,—nothing more: he has expressed his own observations, his own fancies, his own feelings, and they are such, though often rudely, unskilfully, and sometimes obscurely expressed, as to show that he has been gifted with the eye, and the ear, and the feeling of a poet: the art is wanting, and it is now too late for him to acquire it.

No other alterations have been made in his pieces than by occasional omissions, sometimes altering a word in such cases for the sake of connection,—and by correcting a very few grammatical errors.

I would have said something here concerning the March of Intellect, and the beneficial direction which might be given it by those who are not for beating it to the tune of Ça ira. But I shall have other opportunity for this, and it is now time that Mr. Jones should speak for himself.

Before I conclude, I must, however, in my own behalf, give notice to all whom it may concern, that I, Robert Southey, Poet Laureate, being somewhat advanced in years, and having business enough of my own fully to occupy as much time as can be devoted to it, consistently with a due regard to health, do hereby decline perusing or inspecting any manuscript from any person whatsoever, and desire that no application on that score may be made to me from this time forth; this resolution, which for most just cause is taken and here notified, being, like the laws of the Medes and the Persians, not to be changed.

Also, I give notice, that I have entered into a society for the discouragement of autograph collectors; which society will not be dissolved till the legislature in its wisdom shall take measures for suppressing that troublesome and increasing sect.

Lastly, I shall be obliged to those journals which will have the kindness to make these notices more widely known. And if my county member, Sir James Graham, would be pleased to mention them in the House of Commons,—which he may do with as much propriety as when he spoke of the same person there on a former occasion,—they would then have the advantage of being taken down by the reporters, inserted in all the daily newspapers, copied into the weekly and provincial ones, and finally recorded in the Parliamentary Debates.

ATTEMPTS IN VERSE,

BY

JOHN JONES,

AN OLD SERVANT;

WITH

AN ACCOUNT OF HIS LIFE,

WRITTEN BY HIMSELF.

TO

ROBERT SOUTHEY, ESQ.

———◆———

THE place of my birth, Sir, which happened in January, 1774, was the village of Clearwell, in Newland, in that part of Gloucestershire called the Forest of Dean. My father, Sir, from the period to which my memory extends until the time of his death, was employed in the gardens of Charles Edwin, Esq., father of the late Thomas Wyndham, Esq., many years M.P. for Glamorganshire; my mother kept a small shop in the village, in which I was useful to her, at a very early age, in going to and fro to Monmouth, about six miles distance, for the necessaries required in her little way of business. This I must have commenced doing when little more than seven years of age, up to which period I had been a short time at school, to an old woman, with whom I learnt my letters and spelling, but I believe I made but little progress in reading. The only person in the village who taught writing at that time was an old man, by trade a stone-cutter, and he only on winter evenings—after his return from his daily labour; to him I went the best part of two winters, and that, Sir, was the finishing of my education. At the age of ten I was engaged to drive plough at the 'squire's, and at different places, and continued that kind of employment for four years; and up to this period, Sir, I do not recollect to have read in any book but the Psalter and Testament, and sometimes a chapter in the Bible, by reading verses alternately with other boys: but with the little money that came into my possession I purchased songs—the Mournful Lady's Garland, and such stories as are generally hawked about in a pedlar's basket, and which I was very fond of reading, and was often affected to tears by them. At the age of fourteen, Sir, I went to a friend of my father's, who kept a small inn, in Chepstow, where I remained about three years, during which time I was very actively employed, and do not remember to have made any advance in reading or writing; but at the end of that time, having had many small sums given me, I was in possession of four guineas, and with that, Sir, I set off for Bath, where I had a cousin who had been many years a servant there, and who was very kind to me, and soon procured me a place as foot-boy; and Mrs. Edwin being at that time in Bath, was so good as to say what she knew of me, which proved to be satisfactory in point of character. The family consisted of two ladies only, and I had an old Frenchman over me as butler; and it being about the time that the French Revolution commenced, he was very interested in the politics of the day, and frequently went out soon after breakfast and returned but a short time before dinner; therefore, Sir, I had to lay the cloth and to place every thing in readiness by the time he came home; this I used to do an hour or two before the necessary time, for there was a book-case in the dining-room which was left open, and by this means I was enabled to spend many a delightful hour at it; and as plays were what mostly engaged my attention at that time, and Shakespeare's being in the collection, I read the whole of them, and some of them twice over; and when I could not be in the dining-room I read in the Bible below stairs, and, I believe, went regularly through it; but the history of Joseph, Ruth, and some other parts, pleasing me most, I read those passages many times over. At the end of two years I engaged myself with a lady who only kept myself and two female servants, but here, Sir, I had nothing to read; but as I found I had improved myself in reading, it occurred to me, Sir, that I ought to do something in writing, and nothing less than an attempt to write a play could content me; and big with the idea of such an undertaking, I hurried away to the stationer's, and expended almost all my money in the purchase of a dictionary, paper, pens, &c., but having no place to myself, and being desirous that no person should be made acquainted with my intention, and having only my bed-room in the garret to retire to, and that being out of the reach of the sound of the bell, I could do but little at it; but I finished it before I left my situation, in which I staid two years. I then went to see my friends, Sir, and took it with me; and I paid my old schoolmaster, the stone-cutter, for writing it out for me, reading it out to him as he proceeded, for my writing no person could read but myself, and when done, Sir, he thought it such a marvellous thing for a boy who had only been a few winter evenings to school to him, and praised it so much, that I was induced to send it off by the coach to London, directing it to the manager of the Haymarket Theatre; and after a long time, Sir, I received a letter, and I wonder now at the forbearance with which it was written, giving me the information that it would not do for representation, and advising me not to spend my time in such difficult undertakings; but I could hardly bring myself to believe that they had not copied it off, or stole the plot, or played me some dirty trick in it. In those proceedings, Sir, which I have kept a profound secret from that time until the present moment, I spent all my money, and then set off for Bath in search of another situation, and that I might avoid ridicule I destroyed my play, and the only part of it that remains on my memory is the following song or glee, which I had put into the mouths of some soldiers just before entering on the field of battle.

"Come, come, my boys, let's prepare to meet the foe,
Come, come, my boys, let's drink before we go;
When in battle, cannons rattle, we can't do so.
Here, good, good, good, may the bottle go,
There, pop, and off our noddles go.
And when we're there, we shall not fare,
As we do here, taking good cheer
Through the sweet brown lips of a bottle-O;
Then come, come, come, let's drink, drink, drink,
And take good cheer awhile we're here,
Lest, pop, and off our noddles go."

I soon engaged myself again, Sir, with an old gentleman and his three nieces, whose names were Alexander, uncle and sisters of the present Lord Chief Baron, and I had not been in the family many months before, young as I was, I was made upper servant, and as I received a little card money at times, I soon was enabled to procure me some books, which I did by subscribing two or three quarters to the library, and the ladies were very kind to me, and often lent me others, and about this time, Sir, I bought the first and almost the only book of poems I was ever master of, which was called Jane's Beauties, and this I read over several times; but my chief reading now was history, and I made some poetical attempts, but I kept copies of none of them excepting the epitaph on Molly Mutton, an old woman very well known about the streets of Bath at that time; but on some of my verses falling into the hands of the ladies, they were much amused with them, and, I believe, expressed regret that I had not been better educated. The housekeeper, Sir, was very kind to me, and on my expressing sorrow at her departure once when she was going to see her friends, she desired me to write something extempore in which my regret might be more strongly expressed, when in a few minutes I remember putting the following lines into her hand:—

> "There something is, my Martha dear,
>   So amiable about thee,
> The house is Heaven, when thou art here,
>   But Hell to me without thee."

After living with this family five years, Sir, I left them in consequence of their going to reside in Scotland, and unto this hour I remember them with gratitude and respect. This brings me to the year 1800, when I engaged myself with a gentleman of the name of Wynch, who likewise treated me very kindly, and in whose service I attempted to compose a few pieces in verse, chiefly songs, two of which only I put in my book, and one of those you have marked for transcription; I have two or three others in my memory, which, perhaps, Sir, I may send for your opinion. From Mr. Wynch, I went to Mr. Lynch, with whom I went to Ireland; but not liking that country I left him, Sir, in about a year and three or four months, but he was a kind and indulgent master and was unwilling to part with me; and in a letter of recommendation which he gave me, he was pleased to say that my conduct had not in a single instance been otherwise than he could have wished it to have been; and with that character, Sir, I entered into the family which I am now serving, in January, 1804, and have continued in it first, with the father, and then with the son, only during an interval of eighteen months, up to the present hour; and during which period most of my trifles have been composed, and some of my former attempts brought (perhaps) a little nearer perfection; but I have seldom sat down to study any thing, for in many instances when I have done so a ring at the bell, or a knock at the door, or something or other, would disturb me, and not wishing to be seen, I frequently used to either crumple my paper up in my pocket, or take the trouble to lock it up, and before I could arrange it again, I was often, Sir, again disturbed; from this, Sir, I got into the habit of trusting entirely to my memory, and most of my little pieces have been completed and borne in mind for weeks before I have committed them to paper; from this I am led to believe that there are but few situations in life in which attempts of the kind may not be made under less discouraging circumstances. Having a wife and three children to support, Sir, I have had some little difficulties to contend with, but, thank God, I have encountered them pretty well; I have received many little helps from the family, for which I hope, Sir, I may be allowed to say, that I have shown my gratitude by a faithful discharge of my duty; but within the last year my children have all gone to service. Having been rather busy this last week, Sir, I have taken up but little time in the preparation of this, and I am fearful you will think it comes before you in a discreditable shape, but I hope you will be able to collect from it all that may be required for your benevolent purpose; but should you wish to be empowered to speak with greater confidence of my character, by having the testimony of others in support of my own, I believe, Sir, I should not find much difficulty in obtaining it; for it affords me some little gratification, Sir, to think that in the few families I have served, I have lived respected, for in none do I remember of ever being accused of an immoral action, nor with all my propensity to rhyme, have I been charged with a neglect of duty. I therefore hope, Sir, that if some of the fruits of my humble muse be destined to see the light, and should not be thought worthy of commendation, no person of a beneficent disposition will regret any little encouragement given to an old servant under such circumstances; but above all, Sir, I hope there will be found no person so ill-natured as to upbraid you for the part you have taken in their introduction, when it is done from motives the most kind and disinterested. I will endeavour, Sir, to let you have the verses by the time you wish, and will do my best to improve them; but as yet I have said but little to any person respecting them, and I believe, Sir, I must not address my friends on the subject, until I again trespass on your kindness for instructions how to proceed, for which Sir, there can be no hurry.

 Believe me, Sir,
  Your most obliged
   and most grateful servant,
    JOHN JONES.

Kirkby Hall,
August 15th, 1827.

THE AUTHOR TO HIS BOOK.

Poor rugged offspring of my humble Muse,
The world may spurn thee, and thy faults abuse;
For in thy progress not a peaceful hour
Had I to form thee, and no classic power;
Plain simple Nature, in her homely way,
With sudden impulse sung each artless lay,
To state her feelings, or express a thought
Of what her knowledge or her fancy caught;
No state of ease the hapless Muse enjoyed,
The hands were busy, and the ears annoyed
By those quick sounds with which the tongues are rife,
Of mortals bustling in domestic life.
For far from sounds of strife and noisy mirth.
Doth Fancy love to give her musings birth.
Nursed in a soil which felt no cheering rays,
And laughter fearing, without hope of praise,
Nor on thee having leisure to bestow,
Thou wert uncherished, and thy growth was slow;
But when through time some incident arose
That called the heart to pleasure or to woes,
Which Nature kindly asked the Muse to paint,
Her willing fervor broke through all restraint,

And soon depicted what the bosom felt,
And then to thee some little substance dealt.
Loved child of fancy! not endeared for worth,
But as a toy to him who gave thee birth,
Not oft intruded on another's view,
Few of thy nature or existence knew,
And when beheld, opinions, coldly given,
Still chilled the source by which thou might'st have
    thriven.

But on thee chance beamed a more genial ray,
Which lit and led thee into Southey's way;
And he saw even in thy small share of skill,
That there was in thee something pleasing still,
Where those who met thee with a nature kind
Might some congenial charm, amusing find;
And at the risk of every critic's strife,
He lends his hand to lead thee into life,
For which I'll nurse, whate'er my fate may be,
A grateful thought to life's extremity.

To help thee forward, when thou first could'st run,
Some promised stoutly, but have little done;
Others, whose strains came in a softer swell,
Found kindred spirits, and have served thee well;
For every kindness, be it great or small,
I feel most grateful, and, I thank them all.

THE JOURNEY OF LIFE.

The Journey of Life
There are none can presage;
From all we can learn
'Tis an uncertain stage;
If short or extended,
No mortal can say,
What up-hills or down-hills
There are in the way;
Yet were all we travellers
Social inclined,
And true honest hearted,
And loving and kind;
Nor man to man scornful,
Nor man to man wrong,
How happily we might
All travel along!
But Pow'r will oppress thee,
And Pride pass thee by,
And Folly will laugh
At a tear in thine eye;

And, should dark misfortune
Thy prospects o'ercast,
E'en Friendship will leave thee
Exposed to the blast;
And Envy and Malice
Augment thy distress;
And Cunning and Avarice
Thy little make less.
But, strengthen'd by Virtue,
Still bravely contend,
And Hope will uphold thee,
And God be thy friend.

THE SNOWBALL.

I heard the wint'ry north winds blow,
   One dreary, cold, and cheerless night,
And thickly fell large flakes of snow,
   Which clothed the world in spotless white.

When morn awoke, it seem'd to say,
   " I'm dawning forth a day of woe,
The birds shall know nor vacant spray,
   Nor what to do, nor where to go."

I slowly beat my trackless way,
   The walk, the garden's summit sought,
Contemplating the scene to-day
   The last unconscious night had wrought.

The fallow brown, the verdant mead,
   And rugged heath within my view,
Had lost their charms; o'er all was spread
   A robe of one unvaried hue.

"Here look," I said, " ye proud, and know,
   As these are now, in semblance seen
And undistinguish'd in the snow,
   You'll be—beneath a turf of green.

" The snow shall yield to milder skies,
   The fields their genial hue shall wear;
But when from earth your spirits rise,
   The poor as comely forms shall bear."

With musings thus my mind was fraught,
   When faintly gleam'd the rising sun,
An airy wish my fancy caught,
   A ball of snow it fixt upon.

Elated by a childish pride
   I wound a snowball round and high,
And more than once I turn'd aside
   To shun the gaze of passers by.

How oft, what men alone enjoy,
   Their public precepts seem to chide;
How prone was I to play the boy,
   But wish'd, proud world, from thee to hide.

Dost thou man's guileless foibles see?
  Those, in thine ire, thou'lt magnify,
Attach them to some obloquy,
  And damn them in the public eye.

Sweet virtue's sober, chaste career,
  Dost thou in wanton sport molest,
Nor pity's tender, balmy tear,
  Falls uninsulted by thy jest!

When ponderous grown, I view'd with care
  My fancy's child, so fondly rear'd,
And found, tho' erst it shone so fair,
  'Twas now impure, and unendear'd.

Its progress tracing from its birth
  In every turn it made to power,
It bore oppressive on the earth,
  And crush'd the root of many a flower.

Does man not more oppression show
  In every turn from low degree?
Yes, yes, my pompous ball of snow,
  Strong semblance of the world's in thee!

This flow'ry tribe, to thee a prey,
  Alas! to these, with longing eyes,
Some mind congenial oft may stray,
  In hope to view their offspring rise;

But, maim'd and bare, in vain the spring
  Shall come their verdure to restore;
In vain each shower refreshment bring,
  They'll rear on earth their heads no more.

Bedeck'd no more in lovely hue,
  The breath no more their sweets inhale,
The longing eye no flower shall view,
  And on their charms no bee regale.

But why, cold lump, to thee declaim,
  Or why, ye flowers, your fate deplore,
When suff'ring souls my pity claim,
  And real woes deserve it more?

Of those who range yon heights sublime,
  Where splendour Fortune's idols show,
Are some, man marvels how they climb,
  Emerg'd from indigence below.

Could he their tracks, as thine, behold,
  Congenial crimes his eye might meet,
And many a flower of mortal mould
  Untimely crush'd beneath his feet.

Ambition rears the buoyant head,
  And pride, in power, is slow to spare;
On those they pass, in scorn, they tread
  With all the mighty pomp they bear.

As thine, the Miser's heart is cold,
  Destructive each of Nature's plan;
Thou, earth, and he, imprisons gold,
  The food of flowers and staff of man.

Increase of gold adds might to power,
  And vice more strong augmenteth woe,
He'll catch the drops of every shower
  And stagnate streams Heav'n meant should flow.

Oh! could but these his channels shun,
  And branch in streamlets unconfined,
Some would in generous courses run,
  And draughts of comfort yield mankind.

Tho' pity leaves no plaint unsung,
　　Though misery bleeds at every pore,
He'll mock the tale of either tongue,
　　And turn them weeping from the door.

Soon he, like thee, shall disappear,
　　Attended by no child of woe;
Where Virtue's children shed a tear,
　　His children's tears shall cease to flow.'

And, torn from life, what tongue shall say,
　　Or how he fares, or where may dwell?
None e'er from hence the scene survey,
　　And none that see will ever tell.

But thank thee well, for what I know;
　　My bosom's yearning with desire
Of what thou'st taught me in the snow,
　　My friend, to tell beside the fire.

Near stream'd the Mole, close at its brink
　　Arose a cot of neat degree;
I heard, methought, the wicket clink,
　　And, led by fancy, went to see.

Its humble tenant met my sight,
  (How chance, sometimes, strange things will
    do!)
The hair that crown'd his head was white—
  The name he bore—was Snowball, too.

His cheeks the bloom of health had on,
  His form the prime of life array'd;
A smile, which on his features shone,
  Of death no tardy thoughts betray'd.

Sweet sprightly souls, all flaxen-brow'd,
  Around their sire young antics wrought;
To each a willing head he bow'd,
  Whose lips a parting kiss besought.

From man to snow my fancy sped,
  And still what sage, methought, can say—
(Though hope with years the mortal fed,)
  Which first shall pass, of these, away?

The leaves, but on the spray, we see,
  Our knowledge o'er their course extends;
And man in life to-day may be,
  But there of him our knowledge ends.

By passions strong, when reason's blind,
   He's led until the blow be given;
When lo! his passport's left unsigned,
   And closed he'll find the gates of Heaven.

What stores the ant and bee provide,
   When leaves and blossoms clothe the boughs;
Oh! Man, with all thy sense and pride,
   How much outdone art thou by those!

Now fast the snow was seen to shrink,
   And Nature's face more gay to beam,
And what the earth refused to drink,
   Wound slowly on and join'd the stream.

But lingering there, my snowball stood,
   Till many suns stole down the sky;
A remnant yet escaped the flood,
   When pass'd the sexton, mournful, by.

" Ho! man," said I, " why bow thine head?
   That step so slow, and brow of care,
Says thou, a meddler with the dead,
   Of woes must no light burthen bear.

" With unconcern, by sorrow's side,
 Aye, with the sod just drench'd with tears,
Thou'rt seen, from love's fond eye to hide
 Of life the pride, and joy of years."

" In vain," said he, " those tears are shed;
 'Tis meet on death the sod should close,
And grief 'twould be to spirits fled,
 Could love recall them from repose.

" Since, weary of the world's caprice,
 Man here in murmurs dire complains,
Why mourn, when he shall pass where bliss
 In every sweet perfection reigns?

" Tho' in thy path Fate's webs be spun
 Which catch thy every hope that flies,
If well thy earthly task be done,
 Thou yet a blissful soul shalt rise.

" But haste, for time speeds fast on wings,
 Whilst man is reckless, slow, or gay,
Tho' oft some kind alarum rings,
 To warn him of the coming day,

" Heaven oft a shaft abruptly sends,
 Its power a wayward world to show;
E'en now, from whence yon smoke ascends,
 Is mourn'd an unexpected blow.

" And closed are eyes the morn awoke;
 To other realms a spirit's fled;
This hour hath dealt the fatal stroke,
 And Snowball's stretch'd on death's cold bed.

" But, rest our plaintive converse here,
 To toll his mournful knell I'm bound,
Soon, on the breeze, thy pensive ear
 Will note its deep and solemn sound."

My trembling heart beat in my breast
 To think, when pondering o'er death's hour,
That he, who did the thought suggest,
 Should bow so soon beneath its power.

Those tender souls, who skipp'd with pride,
 To share his smile around the door,
Nor saw that death lurk'd by his side,
 Nor thought that soon he'd smile no more.

Man, think, what e'er thy state reveals—
   Youth, health, or strength, these all had he;
Yet, then was Death close at his heels,
   And now as close to thine may be.

On this reflection prone to dwell,
   I, to and fro, the walk paced on,
Oft murmuring, as I heard the knell,
   " Yes! ere the snow, poor Snowball's gone!"

WHY THAT SIGH, &c.

Why that sigh art thou suppressing,
  Did it take its flight from grief?
Yes, that rising tear's confessing
  Thou art pain'd, and need'st relief.

To my mental vision show it,
  Fear thee not to trouble me;
'Twill less painful be to know it,
  Than what dumb suspense will be.

If some pregnant cloud appals thee,
  Love may shield thee from the shower;
If perplexing cares inthral thee,
  Counsel may dispel their power.

If reflection doth remind thee
  Of the fleeting state of breath,
And of one thou'st left behind thee
  In the darksome shades of death,

Once the idol of affection,
   Once the joy of youthful years,
One to whom sweet recollection
   Pays those tributary tears,

Pure's the grateful spring that fed them,
   Down their channels let them steal,
'Tis a pensive bliss to shed them,
   Which the virtuous, only, feel.

If thou'st view'd some scene before thee,
   Which in fancy's overcast,
And thou fear'st the kind beam o'er thee
   Will not light thee to the last,

Let such prospects ne'er deject thee,
   Be they dark, or be they clear;
That a guide will e'er direct thee,
   Never doubt, and never fear.

LINES

ADDRESSED

TO MRS. LAWRENCE, STUDLEY PARK, YORKSHIRE.

On New Year's Day, 1824.

Oh! Lady of Studley, resplendent in worth
   Is the Star which on thee its mild influence beams,
Attracted by virtue, when bright'ning on earth,
   It play'd on thy breast and dissolved it in streams.
And ceaseless and pure, from the heart-springs they flow,
   The channels of pity they love to explore,
And many a comfort they yield as they go,
   To the aged, the weary, the care-worn and poor.

Oh! Lady, 'tis sweet in the bye-path to tread
   Which leadeth to penury's door,
To succour the ailing, and pillow the head
   Which had not a pillow before;
To cherish the widow; the orphan protect,
   Whom death of its guides has despoiled,
And train it to knowledge, and teach it respect,
   And rear it a virtuous child.

And, Lady, 'tis sweet to the bounteous soul,
   Which prides in the good it can do,
To have such resources within its controul,
   As Heaven hath measured to you.
And may they increase, still empowering the will
   To solace affliction in tears,
Whilst He who discerns how your trusts you fulfil,
   Awards you health, honour, and years.

This day to a bantling hath Time given birth,
   Which bears the Omnipotent's plan,
As well as the various changes of earth,
   The yearly allotment of man.
That its portion for you may be tempered as sweet
   As a sensible hope can desire,
Is the wish of a soul to whom hope is a cheat,
   The poor humble bard you inspire.

A VOICE FROM RIPON.
January 1, 1825.

Full fast came the herald, from Studley's bowers,
   Of our Lady's danger informing,
And fear made sad our evening hours,
   Tho' gay had we been in the morning.

A night's repose, in suspense, we sought,
   But none took we for sorrow,
Our sleep was chased by the restless thought
   Of what might be on the morrow.

When the morning beam'd and in the west
   Inquiring looks we were casting,
How oft our mental tongues express'd,
   " May the life of our Lady be lasting!"

But from the west we no tidings gain'd
   But what despair indited,
Not a thought had we that was not pain'd,
   Not a hope that was not blighted.

'Till, sweet as the morning ray appears
   To the night-bewildered stranger,
A sound broke forth on our pensive ears,
   That lessen'd our Lady's danger.

And now, as reviving nature glows
   In spring, when the sun grows stronger,
We joy in the love our Ruler shows
   In the meed of our Lady longer.

Tho' bridal'd not, and children none,
   To many has she been a mother,
And when to the regions of bliss she's gone,
   We shall see not such another.

Like her, ye more reckless, whom fortune befriends,
   Have an eye to the prospect before ye;
She dispenses the blessings which Heaven sends,
   In paving her way to its glory.

The gloom of sorrow that sate on each brow
   Declared with what grief we should mourn her;
And the pleasure that brightens each countenance
      now,
   Is light to the love which is borne her.

DEEP IN THE DELL.

Deep in the dell, when pensive straying,
    Far from every noisy sound,
I saw a spring in beauty playing
    From a rock with foliage crowned;
And as its airy bound 'twas taking,
    And its form a radiance shed,
A crag beneath, the torrent breaking,
    Around in parting streams it spread.

And each a channel lonely winding,
    Dull and slowly seem'd to run,
And turn'd, methought, in hope of finding
    That with which its course begun;
From either side to each inclining,
    One by one, the current fed;
Fast it flowed, when all combining,
    Praises murmuring as it sped.

'Twas like, methought, two souls existing,
    Young in years and light in care,
When in social bands enlisting,
    Life is sweet, and hope is fair.
Joys, which mutual love provides them,
    Cheer their course, and on they go
Till some turn of fate divides them,
    Strange and dreary ways to know.

In lonely hours, anticipation
    Paints the scene of joys to come;
And when 'tis view'd, how inclination
    Woos the path which leads to home,
And when those souls, in memory chaptered,
    The seat of love's attraction swell,
Congenial spirits flow enraptured,
    Like the waters down the dell.

AN ADDRESS TO A DEAD CAT,

WHICH HAD FALLEN FROM THE IVY-TREE THAT RUNS UP THE TOWER OF KIRKBY FLEETHAM CHURCH, YORKSHIRE; UP WHICH IT IS SUPPOSED IT HAD CLIMBED AFTER BIRDS.

Wert thou by mad ambition fired,
Or wert by sensual hopes inspired?—
But, by whatever thou on wert led
It matters not, life's spark is fled.

I ween the fluttering tribe above
In airy tumult won thy love,
And, branch by branch, their height to gain,
Thou climb'dst, unconsciously and vain.

When creeping on, thro' foliage green,
In hope by art to rise unseen,
The nearing sounds thy fancy charm'd,
Nor look below thy fears alarm'd.
With cautious step and eye intent,
Surprise thy aim, and ruthless bent,
The height was gained, the birds had fled,
And thou a victim in their stead.

When danger met thy wond'ring eyes,
Most loud and piteous were thy cries,
And pity heard, and breathed a sigh,
And grieved she could not climb so high.

On faithless boughs, unyielding rest,
When weary morn and hunger prest,
A blast most rude the branches tost,
Thy hold exhausted nature lost,
And down to earth impetuous sent:
In cries and groans thy life was spent.

Had to thy wants no heed been shown,
And thou the pangs of hunger known,
And urged on by a sense so keen,
More piteous would thy fate have been;
For life will waste on stinted fare,
And life is first in nature's care.

But ever wont wert thou to find,
Of food thy fill, a welcome kind,
And daily in thy peaceful dome
Wert petted, stroked, and call'd poor Tom!
To please thee, too, 'twas the resort
Of cats, for play,—and mice for sport.

With comforts thus, strewn in thy way,
Less prone thou should'st have been to stray,
And not indulgence sought in strife,
And led a wild advent'rous life;
But life hath for thy errors paid,
And low thy daring spirit's laid.

Did passions, Tom, to thine a-kin,
But prompt alone thy race to sin,
How many hearts, with woe oppress'd,
How many sighs, which pain the breast,
How many bitter tears that flow,
Had mortals ne'er been doom'd to know,
Whom none can cheer, and nought console,—
For forms, who risk, with life, a soul!

There are—(a wanton course to run,)
Those who a home and bliss will shun;
But gone, alas! within the door
The sweets of bliss are felt no more,
But to the threshhold may be traced
From every scene the wanderer's paced,
Where Riot sung, or Folly played,—
A path by evil tidings made,—

And on 'tis trode, without a turn,
Till deep for woe a channel's worn.
It fills! it streams! a flood appears!
And all the dome's deluged with tears.

At worth's expense their passions fed,
They're soon to vice from folly led,
Desires,—increasing every hour,
As streams augment by every shower,
And pamper'd till they're tyrants grown,—
Subdue each power, and wield their own;
They seek their food by stealth or strife,
Offend the laws, and forfeit life.

Too gay in sober life to move,
And envious of the show above,
And vainly will'd to rise like thee,
Will others climb ambition's tree,
And wind, in specious guise, their way,
Thro' branches clothed in bright array,
Ascend its height, by force or guile,
And glare, in glorious pomp, awhile.

But wasting strength will soon betray
Their want of power their hold to stay,

When, with reluctance to depart,
A union's form'd with pride and art,
Who form a tale of pleasing sounds,
And some demure pretext propounds,
And if the snare fresh succours bring,
They yet a little longer cling.

But patient time will truth disclose,
And every art by which they rose,
And suff'ring dupes, with vengeful frown,
A storm will raise, and shake them down,
And shame, the second wife of pride,
Will lead them off, in shades to hide.

Would those who climb, and those who stray,
Above their height, and from their way,
A moment pause—to calm the breath,
And ponder o'er thy fall and death,
And let the truths by thee defined
Restrain the wanderings of the mind,
And mould them to a just degree,—
How well, for Men, and Cats, 'twould be!

LINES,

OCCASIONED BY WALKING OVER SOME FALLEN LEAVES.

Fallen leaves, your rustlings waken
   Fancy from a gentle sleep;
Note will of ye now be taken,
   O'er ye as I slowly creep.

Yes, her eyes are backward wending,
   And in early life you're seen
Where kind spring, your race befriending,
   Led ye forth in buds of green.

Now she sees you far advancing,
   To the mild beam opening wide,
Now in gentle zephyrs dancing,
   In your full expanded pride.

In the glory of existence,
   Now you're ey'd from hill and glade,
To the sun ye show resistance,
   And ye yield a cooling shade.

Now a change in life o'ertakes ye,
    And ye wear a golden cast;
Now your charms and strength forsake ye,
    And ye sicken in the blast.

Now from every tree you're spreading,
    Borne away on wind and stream;
On ye now I'm rudely treading,—
    Get ye down to whence ye came.

"Hush!" methinks I hear ye saying,
    "Thine no better doom will be;
Life's tree, on which thou art staying,
    Is a frail unstable tree.

"Many souls now on it number'd,
    In some near approaching squall,
Down shall come, with crime encumber'd,
    And more deep than us may fall.

"Be not with thyself elated;
    Be thou not so proud of birth;
Thou to us art near related,
    Children all of mother Earth.

" Let our frail existence tell thee,
    Thine is but a breath of air,
Soon a puff to earth shall fell thee,
    And with us thou'lt mingle there."

Yes! from earth, we are descended,
    And a-kin, I'll not deny,
Nor that, when my course is ended,
    With you there my frame may lie.

I've a spirit which must leave it
    For eternal pain or ease,
Help me, oh my God, to save it,
    Lest I fall more low than these!

THE BUTTERFLY TO HIS LOVE.

Extend thy wings, my dear,
And we will round the bowers go;
The sun is warm and clear,
And inviting is the day;
The dews have left the blade,
And fragrant now the flowers blow,
And, as they blow to fade,
Let's enjoy them while we may!
We're not of mortal mould
To die, and then unfold
Our eyes in still a brighter world,
Its glories to explore;
Our life is but a summer long;
Then let us rove its sweets among,
For when the blast blows bleak and strong,
We sleep, to wake no more.

TO A WILD HEATH FLOWER.

Sweet flow'ret! from Nature's indulgence thou'rt cast,
Thy home's on the cold heath, thy nurse is the blast,
No shrub spreads its branches to shelter thy form,
Thou'rt shook by the winds, and thou'rt beat by the storm;
But the bird of the moor on thy substance is fed,
And thou giv'st to the hare of the mountain a bed;
In youth, from the cold winds thou'lt grant them a space,
And in age, when the fowler's at war with their race.
The winds may assail thee, the tempest may rage,
Thy nature is proof to the war which they wage;
Thou'lt smile in the conflict, and blossoms unfold,
Where the nurslings of favour would shrink from the cold;
Though rugged and sterile the seat of thy birth,
Simplicity formed thee of beauty and worth.

Remain then, sweet blossom, the pride of the moor,
In loneliness flourish, unpampered and pure,—

Expand in the tempest, and bloom on the brow.
An emblem of sweet independence art thou;
And the soul who beholds thee unhurt in the strife
Shall learn to contend with the troubles of life;
And when the cold wind of adversity's felt,
And the shafts of affliction are ruthfully dealt,
His spirit, unbroken, shall rise to the last,
And his virtues shall open and bloom in the blast,
And his joys shall be sweet when the storm is at rest,
And the sun beams of glory shall play on his breast.

OLD MAWLEY TO HIS ASS.

THE FOLLOWING ACCOUNT OF WHOM APPEARED IN THE SUN NEWSPAPER OF APRIL, 1828.

"An old man died last week at Langport, near Lewes, upwards of eighty years old. He had resided on the family estate of the Tourles nearly fifty years, one of whom bequeathed him an annual income, which he has regularly enjoyed; and from the present head of the family he has received very beneficent attention; on his death-bed he desired that his old donkey, which he had daily strode for forty-five years, should be killed and buried by his side. His general avocation was to look after the rabbits, and the youngsters of several generations have been awed by the call of ' here comes old Mawley,' when they were employed in birds' nesting on the race hill."

TOGETHER we have borne the blast,
For five-and forty winters past,
But we are now both waning fast,
   My poor old Ass.

Our sun is sinking in the west,
By night's dark shades we're closely prest,
And soon shall reach our home of rest,
   My faithful Ass.

A faithful friend thou'st been to me
As ever beast to man could be,
And grateful is my heart to thee,
My good old Ass.

In many a long and daily round
O'er rugged ways and miry ground,
On thee I've ease and comfort found,
My steady Ass.

We've met the storm's tremendous ire,
The thunder's crash and lightnings fire,
And never would'st thou fear or tire,
My patient Ass.

Through rain and hail, and drifting snow,
And winds as keen as Heaven could blow,
Thy willing nature bade thee go,
My gentle Ass.

O'er every rough and slippery road,
With patient care thou'st firmly strode,
And sav'd, more than thyself, thy load,
My worthy Ass.

And in thy long-spent youthful day,
The sprightly pranks thou'st wont to play,
Drew from love's sun a tender ray,
     My merry Ass.

More strong it grew from year to year,
Till time and worth hath made thee dear;
Oft o'er thee now I shed a tear,
     My poor old Ass.

And can I go, when life shall end,
And leave so good and kind a friend,
In cold neglect thy days to end,
     My hapless Ass?

Unhoused by night, by day unfed,
In lonely lanes in mire to tread,
With not to shelter thee a shed,
     My suffering Ass?

How would the ruthless youngsters stride
Thy bare back bones and goad thy side,
And chequer with long stripes thy hide,
     Unhappy Ass!

And thou would'st then a visit pay
To where thou'dst known a better day,
And thence be rudely chased away,
    My injured Ass.

And to be chastened like a thief
Whence hope had led thee for relief,
Would break thy poor old heart with grief,
    My honest Ass.

And from the door should'st slowly creep,
And in some quagmire dank and deep
Thou'dst sink, and take thy long night's sleep,
    My weary Ass.

And must thy doom be so severe?
Oh! no, the thought awakes a tear,
I cannot go and leave thee here,
    My faithful Ass.

The reckless may the thought deride,
The wise, perchance, may gently chide;
But we will moulder side by side,
    My loving Ass.

I'll will, that, at my latest sigh,
Thou, too, some easy death shalt die,
And in one grave we both will lie,
              My own old Ass.

We, in thy youth, associates were,
We've lived an undivided pair,
And so to earth we'll go, and there,
              My kind old Ass,

One stone shall cover thou and me;
And where we lie the world may see,
For this our epitaph shall be,
              My friend and Ass.

EPITAPH.

Oh! stay, a moment here expend,
For here, where thou shalt soon extend,
Lie I, old Mawley, and my friend,
              My faithful Ass.

Hast thou a friend as good as mine,
And gratitude was never thine?
Oh! blush thou then, before its shrine,
              For shame, and pass.

TO THE TONGUE.

Thou herald both of love and ire,
Thou chord of truth—thou arrant liar,
Thou calmer and thou cause of strife,
Thou blessing and thou curse of life,
How doth the power to thee consigned,
In adverse ways affect mankind!

Tuned are thy softest strains to move
Some fair, whose ear's awake to love;
In which such sweets thy art instils,
That every nerve with transport thrills;
And hushed is every thought to sleep.
Which o'er the heart should sentry keep;
And every scene's illumed with rays
That beam from hope on future days,
And on love's stream most sweetly goes,
And thou'rt the fount from whence it flows.

And when from sources pure it springs,
A balm for many a wound it brings,

And many draughts, when woes are rife,
'Twill yield, to cool the thirsts of life;
And ne'er its pleasing powers deny
Till nature sinks and leaves it dry.

But oft it flows from art, and tries
To tempt the taste, and lead the eyes,
And lures some object to the brink,
And fondly urges it to drink,
And, hopeful that its balmy powers
May solace yield in future hours,
The draught is quaft, the error's known,
Repentance comes, and peace is flown,
And in the victim's plaints is sung,—
' Oh! woe betide a guileful tongue.'

Thy sounds break forth in anger loud,
Like thunder from a stormy cloud,
And many souls from sweet repose
Provoke to strife or wake to woes.
When passions strong subdue the sense,
Charged with some vain or vile pretence,
Thou deal'st thy harsh invective round,
And every softer voice is drown'd:
The gentle fear, the wise retreat,
And poor dependents mourn their state.

So hard, when laden low, to be
Beneath their load reviled by thee.

As on life's rugged road they tread,
To earn, before they eat, their bread;
When hard they toil and keen their pains,
Their comforts few, and small their gains;
Oh! wouldst thou, with thy kindest powers,
Direct them in their arduous hours,
And rule the weak with mild control,
And ease the heavy burthen'd soul,
And tell them that they're task'd on earth
To try their patience and their worth,
And they who best its trouble bear
Will merit most kind Heaven's care.

Oh! then, illumed with hope's mild ray,
Through life's hard, toilsome, gloomy day,
They'd journey on with hearts more light,
And peaceful lay them down at night.

If thus, what tears would cease to flow,
What pangs their hearts would cease to know,
How many troubled thoughts would rest,
What murmurs would be unexpressed!

When in the cause of truth thou'rt heard,
Thy sounds are sweet in every word,
On virtue's ear they kindly swell,
And where they rise she loves to dwell.
Through life's gay scenes, where folly tries
To win the gaze of youthful eyes,
Where art might lure and vice betray,
They guide her on her lovely way,
To that high eminence of years,
Which rises o'er the vale of fears,
From whence the mind, when backward cast,
Grows pleased to view the dangers past.

When falsehood's tales thou'rt prone to tell,
In loathsome shades thou'rt doom'd to dwell,
And shunn'd thy haunts, thy counsels spurn'd,
Nor ear of worth is to thee turn'd;
And aught of good, or aught of ill,
To lure or shun, as suits thy will,
Thou'lt spread with art what vice may plot,
And those deceive who know thee not;
And should mistrust proclaim thy shame,
Thou'lt shift, with dexterous skill, the blame,
And some poor guileless soul revile,
And from it turn love's stream awhile.

But when the misty scene grows clear
And truth's discern'd, dost thou appear
A thing clad in the world's disgust,
Whom none can love and none will trust.

And when, in penury or pain,
Woe bids thee sound her plaintive strain,
And thou and an assisting tear
Meet,—that the eye and thou, the ear
Of pity,—thy pathetic lay
Through her soft nature pleads its way,
And gains her heart, where deep distress
Finds consolation and redress.

And should the aid to suffering dealt
Be in some needful moment felt,
Reflection comes, to soothe the mind
With charms of every pleasing kind.

When wrath seems kindling in the breast,
By murmurs only yet expressed,
Would'st thou in patient stillness bide,
And let the ruffled thought subside,
Or with, if thou must needs be heard
In thy defence, a soothing word

With reason tempered, stay the strife
That might, if dared, endanger life,
Oh! haply, in a moment's gleam,
Where scowl'd a frown, a smile might beam,
Perchance outheld, for pity's sake,
A hand that 'twould be joy to shake.

Should'st thou with daring meet the shower,
And to a storm provoke its power,
That storm might to a tempest grow,
And reason, the mind's rudder, go,
And passions high, like billows run;
And ere the dreadful strife was done,
Life's bark might on a rock be tost,
And in the wreck a soul be lost;
And many, suffering by the strife,
Would brand thee as the curse of life.

Methinks I hear thee mercy crave,
For thou art but the passions' slave.
Then go, but with respect, from me,
And tell them what I've told to thee.

TO LYDIA,

WITH A COLOURED EGG, ON EASTER MONDAY.

In Scotia so fair, 'tis a custom they say,
   Old Time hath brought down with his stream,
Each friend to present with an egg on this day,
   As a token of love or esteem.

But why or wherefore, is a matter, I wot,
   Tradition withholds from my view,
And since the original cause I have not,
   I'll brood over this for one new.

It bears, my dear Lyd, when minutely defined,
   A fanciful semblance of thee,
Thy heart is its centre, its white is thy mind,
   Its shell and thine honour agree.

If once, from neglect, an egg falls to the ground,
   No art can its virtue restore;
If once at its post honour's not to be found,
   We look there for honour no more.

Since honour's defection will virtue expose,
   And bliss with its purity dwells,
The treasure within thy fair bosom enclose,
   As eggs are enclosed in their shells.

HARK! HARK! &c.

Hark! hark! sweetly the nightingale
Sings, as the moon's peeping over the mountain;
Hark! hark! through the soft evening gale,
How her notes swell from the tree by the fountain;
  Her coming is cheering,
  The summer is nearing,
Sweet nature is smiling, and spring warmly glowing,
  And early to greet them,
  My love and I'll meet them
Adown in the vale where the primrose is blowing.

Hark! hark! still hear the nightingale
Sing, on the lake as the moon's brightly beaming;
Hark! hark! now her notes on the gale
Come from the dell where the water is streaming;
  The verdure is springing,
  The airy choir singing,
The flowers will bloom and their fragrance be shedding,
  Arise, nor be loathful,
  Ye sleepy and slothful,
And view, when the morn beams, the sweets that are
  spreading.

Hark! hark! still sings the nightingale,
Whilst a dark cloud is the moon's rays confining;
Hark! hark! now her voice on the gale
Comes from the brake where the woodbine's entwining;
  The summer is coming,
  The insects are humming,
All nature's expanding in beauty and order;
  My love and I'll wander
  Where streamlets meander,
And where the blue violets bloom on their border.

TO ELIZA,

WITH A LITTLE GOLD KEY.

Eliza, this ring I'll entrust to thy care,
   If thou wilt of the charge but approve,
The worth it encloses thou only shalt share,
   'Tis the key of my heart and its love.

If fortune should from thee its blessings withstay,
   Oh! come in the sorrowful hour,
'Twill open a bosom sincere as the day,
   That will solace thee all in its power.

A few chosen souls have the means of access,
   And friendship and kindness may free,
But I have enclosed in a private recess
   What shall only be opened to thee.

THE FRIEND OF MY HEART.

When my heart droops under worldly displeasure,
And restless emotions its comforts destroy,
In friendship is found a resource beyond measure,
For chasing the cares which the bosom annoy.
Sweet counsel addressing, each moral impressing,
Bestowing each blessing the mind can impart—
Oh! fate, let thy dictates be e'er so distressing,
Preserve for me ever the friend of my heart.

So when the wild storm has disturbed the main ocean,
And peril and toil have the seaman oppressed,
A calm soon, like friendship, shall still its emotion,
And lull, in soft slumbers, his bosom to rest.
Tho' dangers surrounding, and troubles confounding,
If friendship's abounding, 'twill solace impart.
Oh! fate, let thy arrows be ever so wounding,
Preserve for me ever the friend of my heart.

The mortal advancing his own pleasures only,
From whose frigid bosom no sympathy flows,
Shall pass thro', unpitied, unsheltered, and lonely,
The wild and bleak storms, when adversity blows;
No love shall caress him, no friend shall address him,
Tho' care may oppress him and wound like a dart.
Oh! fate, let my prospects be e'er so depressing,
Preserve to me ever the friend of my heart.

MARY KILLCROW.

In the hamlet, where time introduced me to light,
A poor little pitiful stranger on earth,
Till nurs'd with affection, and kiss'd with delight,
And cherish'd by her whom I pain'd at my birth,
Rose sounds which now often resound in mine ears,
And objects which fancy attached to the mind,
And memory hath borne through the tempests of
    years,
Whilst things of more import fell listless behind;
And out of its relics it loveth to show
A dapper old woman named Mary Killcrow.

Two asses had Mary, with saddles and sacks,
And cheerfully with them she trudged through the
    mire,
And twice in the day, with these full on their backs,
They bore from the coalpit our fuel for fire.
Her body was wrapp'd in a mantle of grey,
By a kerchief of blue was her bonnet confined,
And a staff in her hand, if her asses should stray,
With a point in the end, to reprove them behind:

But seldom they felt or a prick or a blow,
So mild was the nature of Mary Killcrow.

The features of Mary were ruffled with age,
And faded her beauties, whatever they were;
The sun in its strength, and the storm in its rage,
Had rendered her brown, had she ever been fair.
Her figure was round, and her stature was low,
And sturdy her limbs, but to quickness inclin'd;
And Mary oft trode the first track in the snow,
With a rude band of hay round each ancle en-
    twin'd.
If wont some defects thy exterior to show,
Rare virtues embellish'd thee, Mary Killcrow.

The male ass was Ned, and the female was Bess;
She oft for their sustenance clipp'd the wild blade,
And ere her own supper she cull'd them a mess,
And ere her own breakfast their hunger was staid:
Their saddles were stuff'd with the softest of hair,
Their beds were composed of the driest of fern;
And many an orphan might wish to lie there,
And there the obdurate might sympathy learn.
There are mothers to children such love never
    show,
As thou didst thine asses, good Mary Killcrow.

The course of her journey wound where, in the dean,
Britannia's best bulwarks in olden time grew,
And ran o'er a common where often was seen
The vilest disturber her peace ever knew.
An ass unrestrain'd there a wanton life led,
And Turk was the name which the libertine bore;
He'd bray after Bess in defiance of Ned,
When woful the fray and appalling the roar;
They'd list not to reason, nor reverence show
To the tongue nor the staff of old Mary Killcrow.

If laden, Ned's burthen soon fell to the ground;
If lighten'd, Ned from her more speedily ran;
To what chance might offer poor Bess would be bound:
Whene'er the bold rivals the conflict began,
The onset was hail'd by the sound of each trump;
Teeth, tongue, heels and nostrils, alike unconfin'd,
The might of the jaws and the strength of the rump
Were rudely enforc'd, or before or behind;
Bess oft gave a leer, and oft with it would go
The sad lamentations of Mary Killcrow.

Disadvantaged was Ned, was each circumstance weigh'd,
For toil and accoutrements straighten'd each joint;
But Mary was kind, and oft sent to his aid
A stroke with her staff or a thrust with her point.
The vanquished would run and the victor would bray,
Whilst Mary from Turk stood the guardian of Bess;
And there must she stand, from the end of the fray,
Till mortal came by to relieve her distress:
No neighbour around thee thy troubles would know,
And haste not to succour thee, Mary Killcrow.

Assistance derived and disasters redress'd,
Poor Mary, departing, would brandish her goad;
But lest her disturber again should molest,
'Twas needful to chase him afar from the road.
He stopp'd with the form, which declin'd to pursue,
And kick'd at the stones which were after him flung;
And when she had dwindled away from his view,
The smart of his wounds would he balm with his tongue.
How oft after crime, when his passions are low,
Man smarts like the ass behind Mary Killcrow.

Poor Mary had journey'd divested of fear,
Had not her vile enemy come by surprize;
But nature had deaden'd the pass to her ear,
Her bonnet contracted the scope of her eyes;
The foe to evade she would often unclose
Her kerchief, when near where the mischief might lurk,
And with her old spectacles striding her nose,
Would take a long look for the dissolute Turk.
There are those who have felt a more dissolute foe,
Than thou and thine asses, good Mary Killcrow.

Thy heart was sincere and thy nature profuse;
Thou would'st brave the rude blast if our fuel should fail,
Nor in the storm's enmity would'st thou refuse
If want chill'd the hearth of one cot in the vale.
Round the hills which enclose it in childhood I wound,
Through the woods which adorn it when older I ranged,
On the hills in its season the primrose I found,
And sloes in the woods when the season was changed;
When winter had whiten'd the summits with snow,
I woo'd the bright coals of old Mary Killcrow.

Heaven sent for thee, Mary, whose wisdom enacts,
That flesh is but dust, and but dust it shall be;
Thine asses are moulder'd, but saddles and sacks
Will long hang in mournful remembrance of thee.
Tho' in the earth's bosom thy wasting form lies,
When angels shall sound the ascension of souls,
Tho' dark was thy calling, thy spirit shall rise
More bright than the flame which arose from thy
    coals.
Ye pious and good, when to Heaven ye go,
You'll see in her glory old Mary Killcrow.

HOME.

I've climb'd the Alpine mountains,
   I've stray'd where Jordan streams,
I've drank of cooling fountains
   In Thibet's sultry beams.
Tho' enterprize impels me
   In distant climes to roam,
Sweet fancy fondly tells me
   The seat of bliss is home.

Each thought's enwrapt in wonder
   When riding on the deep;
The scene enchants me under,
   When standing on the steep.
Some charm in art or nature
   I find where'er I roam,
But none in form or feature
   The heart endears like home.

To rivals I compare thee,
    And, priding in thy worth,
Most sweet's the love I bear thee,
    Thou Isle that gav'st me birth.
Whate'er my cares may chasten
    When far from thee I roam,
I woo the gales to hasten
    The bark that bears me home.

And sweet's the heart's emotion,
    When through the mist appears
The land within the ocean,
    The nurse of early years.
When friends await the greeting,
    The blissful moment's come,
Enraptured is the meeting,
    And sweet the welcome home.

AN ADDRESS TO A VIOLET,

OCCASIONED BY READING THE FOLLOWING LINES IN AN ADDRESS TO THE SAME FLOWER.

" Oh! stay awhile, till warmer showers
And brighter suns shall on thee play."

That thou should'st not thy charms unfold,
And shed thy sweets when winds are cold,
Some reckless mortal bids thee stay
Till milder beams shall on thee play,
To chase the cheerless blast, and warm
Thy lovely, gentle, fragrant form.

Oh! heed thee not the changeful thing;
But come the earliest pride of spring,
And when her robes thy features bear,
Fond love shall come and meet thee there.

And when in lonely glens thou'rt found,
And youth shall tread the fairy ground,
Of soft emotions thou shalt tell
With which their gentle bosoms swell,
When hope is weak, and love is young
And dreads to venture on the tongue.

A meed thou'lt be, when cull'd with care,
To some sweet, blooming, guileless fair;
And as from hand to hand thou'rt past,
The pressure soft—the eye downcast—
The crimson'd blush, and trembling frame,
Will speak of what they dare not name.

And thou shalt in her bosom lie
And move to many a gentle sigh,
And charm the thought and please the breath,
Till thou by love art nurs'd to death.

Should'st thou await a warmer hour
Thou'lt rivals meet in every bower,
Whose pompous forms will shade from view
Thy lowly simple head of blue,
And in the breeze around thee play
In flow'ry pride and colours gay,
And soon the eye allure from thee,
And win the love which thine should be.

But 'tis in specious charms they shine,
That yield no sweets in worth like thine,
But such too oft to favour rise,
Whilst worth, neglected, fades and dies.

Then let thy favour'd form appear
As erst, and when no rival's near;
And still youth's happy emblem prove,
And show the sweets of early love;
And still in glens remote and wild
Be nature's first and sweetest child.

JANE BARNABY.

Jane Barnaby, my dear Jane,
   I'm wearing wan, and old.
As herds at close of eve, Jane,
   Are summon'd to the fold,
I soon to mine shall be, Jane,
   My close of life is near,
And much I need our Shepherd's care,
   Jane Barnaby, my dear.

Jane Barnaby, my dear Jane,
   I'm wearisome on earth,
Nor less in want of aid, Jane,
   Than when I had my birth;
Then with a mother's love, Jane,
   I strengthen'd with the year,
But now I'm fast upon the wane,
   Jane Barnaby, my dear.

Jane Barnaby, my dear Jane,
   Death, terrorless, I see,
My only source of woe, Jane,
   Is lonely leaving thee;
But purity of life, Jane,
   Hath won thee hearts sincere,
And love will yield thee fellowship,
   Jane Barnaby, my dear.

Jane Barnaby, my dear Jane,
   Thy tenderness is sweet,
And grateful is this heart
   That soon will cease to beat.
Thou wert its earliest love, Jane,
   Thou art its solace here,
Thou'lt be its last remembrance,
   Jane Barnaby, my dear.

Jane Barnaby, my dear Jane,
   There's bliss divine in store,
And soft will be the calm, Jane,
   When troubled life is o'er;
Then in my weal rejoice, Jane,
   When I shall disappear,
Nor bathe thy pillow with thy tears,
   Jane Barnaby, my dear.

Jane Barnaby, my dear Jane,
   I go where thou shalt come,
And that shall be our last, Jane,
   Our undivided home.
The painful there shall rest, Jane,
   The weary shall have cheer,
'Tis virtue's sweet Elysium,
   Jane Barnaby, my dear.

Jane Barnaby, my dear Jane,
   Life's flood is ebbing fast,
A few more soft'ning sighs, Jane,
   The shoals will all be past.
To bear my spirit hence, Jane,
   Death's bark is hov'ring near;
Adieu, adieu, a short adieu,
   Jane Barnaby, my dear.

SALLY ROY.

Thou art gentle in thy nature,
   Sally Roy, Sally Roy,
Thou art comely in each feature,
   Sally Roy, Sally Roy,
Thou art sweet, and thou'rt endearing,
Thou art kind, and thou art cheering,
E'er in loveliness appearing,
   Sally Roy, Sally Roy.

As the sun the morning brightens,
   Sally Roy, Sally Roy,
As the moon the evening lightens,
   Sally Roy, Sally Roy,
To the world a light thou'rt lending,
Worth and beauty in it blending,
Oh! thou'rt one of Heaven's sending,
   Sally Roy, Sally Roy.

For the love of thy assistance,
   Sally Roy, Sally Roy,
May'st thou beam thro' my existence,
   Sally Roy, Sally Roy.

Should the cares of life distress me,
With sweet comfort thou'lt address me,
Like an angel sent to bless me,
   Sally Roy, Sally Roy.

Should the frown of fate hang o'er me,
   Sally Roy, Sally Roy,
Should'st thou fade and die before me,
   Sally Roy, Sally Roy,
Oh! the tears of grief will blind me,
In a dark world left behind thee,
Not a ray of hope will find me,
   Sally Roy, Sally Roy.

BY LOVE WE WERE LED, JANE.

By love we were led, Jane,
To woo and to wed, Jane,
To promise, in consort, life's journey to go;
In ailment, in health, Jane,
In want, and in wealth, Jane,
To mingle our portions of pleasure and woe.

As onwards we steal, Jane,
Each turn may reveal, Jane,
Some pleasing allurement to tempt us to stray;
And envy and strife, Jane,
Annoyants of life, Jane,
May ruffle our bosoms, and trouble our way.

And hence 'twill be meet, Jane,
If life shall be sweet, Jane,
With caution and love undivided to steer;
To tread in the road, Jane,
Where prudence hath trode, Jane,
And take at the dwelling of reason our cheer.

  To shun in the crowd, Jane,
  The pert and the proud, Jane,
The vile, and the profligate, mean, and the vain;
  To truth to adhere, Jane,
  And virtue revere, Jane,
That worth may be pleas'd to be seen in our train.

  There are some who may tire, Jane,
  And aidance require, Jane,
And many a bosom affliction may pain;
  O'er those we should bend, Jane,
  And pity extend, Jane,
The sorrowful cheer, and the needy sustain.

  We daily should call, Jane,
  On Him who rules all, Jane,
And render him thanks for the help he hath given;
  Repent, if we have stray'd, Jane,
  And sue for His aid, Jane,
To guide us thro' all the world's mazes to Heav'n.

  If thus we conform, Jane,
  In every rude storm, Jane,
A charm o'er the mind will in stillness console;
  And turning at last, Jane,
  To gaze on the past, Jane,
How sweetly the scene will give cheer to the soul.

A FANCIFUL DESCRIPTION OF A PASSAGE DOWN PART OF THE RIVER WYE, OF A COTTAGE AND ITS INHABITANTS, &c.

A Fragment.

Mid scenes where nature, robed in sweet attire,
Yields charms to please, and grandeur to inspire,
Where fancy grows enraptured as she views,
The Wye her lovely winding course pursues,
Whose airy turns, quick as in sport, delight,
For every turn pours transport on the sight.

High shelving hills in daring forms surprise,
And shade o'er shade in proud progression rise,
Dividing those with gentle slopes between
Vale vale succeeding variegates the scene
Of clustered fields, which teem with waving grain;
Meandering streams fast murmuring for the main,
And lawns and herds, the passing eye admires;
And village churches crown'd with humble spires,
And peeping cots with, pliant to the breeze,
The curling smoke ascending thro' the trees;

And orchards, ranged in uniform array,
In various tints their various fruits display,
And shallows oft admitting thirsty cows,
And staring cow-boys jerking awkward bows.

Oft thro' some space a wild-heath hill is seen,
And lesser hills progressive rise between;
Those groups of herds, in fleecy concourse line,
And blooming whins in yellow spangles shine.
Round some a pass, beguileful of their steeps,
In length'ning windings to the summit creeps;
The traveller there who for his palfry feels,
Dismounting, trails him patient at his heels,
And onward climbs, with palpitating breast,
Whilst fancy dwells on some lov'd spot to rest.
There he is seen, where sweet expansions show
Enchantment spread in nature's lap below.

Of various mansions which those scenes disclose,
Some display industry, and some repose,
The drying net at some low dwelling tells
Where, of the finny race, a scourger dwells;
The farmers shine with neat thatch'd stacks of corn,
Some ancient piles, two sober yews adorn.

Some smile with shrubs, and woven wood-bine bowers,
Where oft the fair are seen midst beds of flowers,
Some humble domes—for show, nor power, nor place,—
Display a useful cultivated space.

Thro' lovely changes thus the eyes are led
To where old Tintern rears its ancient head,
Whose lingering beauties time still leaves behind,
To awe with grandeur and instruct mankind;
In ivy's arms the proud reserve is held,
Whose strong attachment time hath not repell'd.
And still, with zeal the like ne'er man inspired,
'Tis sought in ruin, and in age admired.
Leaving those gems of ancient art behind,
Nature awaits to chase them from the mind,
With all her powers arranged on either shore,
In all the charms of her romantic store.

Stupendous hills the current's course divide,
With trees o'erspread, and branching out in pride,
More bold and grand, some prominently reign,
The sovereigns, and the nobles, in their train,
Some rock breaks forth, and on each winding beams,
As left and right by turns the current streams.

Each side, as each now in arrangement swell,
In soft luxuriance slopes into a dell,
Till winding where, between the opening glades,
The lawns of Piercefield teem with lovely shades;
High on the brow is seen each verdant gleam,
Thence, waving foliage, skirting to the stream,
From trees in seeming strife, all up the steep,
To view their charms reflected in the deep.

Athwart the stream, worn bare by winter storms,
Here cliffs arise in more gigantic forms;
Those tufts of trees in various shades surround,
And minor rocks in many forms abound;
Some from their beds in rugged shape emerge,
And some with foliage crowding on the verge;
Round others torn with elemental strife
Some old trees' roots are creeping after life,
Which still they find, tho' mortal marvels how,
And shed a few gay branches o'er the brow.

The eye to ease, and give the ear its spells,
Sweet Echo here with various handmaids dwells;
Arranged are those for intercourse of sound,
Within communing distances around;
Weary nor listless, ready as they rise,
No sound conveyed her unresounded dies,

But quick, the like, her matchless art returns,
The passing theme the next progressive learns,
So on to each the airy charm is tost,
Until escaping, 'tis in silence lost.

As misers love where vast returns abound,
Here rustics come for interest of sound;
Fond swains are prone to hail their idols whence
The name endeared reverberates on the sense.
Here truant school-boys, ling'ring by the hour,
Sustain reproof, to raise the mimic power;
In sportive mood, respondence to invoke
The sober woodman magnifies his stroke;
The milk-maid's song, the lowing of her cow,
The herdsman's halloo, loit'ring on the brow,
The neighing colts, which o'er their fences peep,
The bleating flocks that browse along the steep,
The sheep-dog's bark, restrictive of their bounds,
The huntsman's horn, the concert of the hounds,
The ploughman's shout when reynard breaks in
      view,
The cracking whips of numbers who pursue,
The crash of fences steeds unmanaged cause,
The bursting laugh each luckless rider draws,
The farmer's ire, whom beasts nor burthens spare,
Affrighted rooks tumultuous in the air,

Are heard and echo'd and re-echo'd here,
Till sweet confusion crowds upon the ear.

There lies between where those high rocks extend,
And whence below expanding groves ascend,
An open space of sweet enchanting ground,
Lovely itself, and charm'd by all around,
Where nature strews beneath the wand'rer's feet
Luxuriant verdure and wild flowers sweet;
Where cluster'd shrubs in wild divisions spread,
Sweet in the breeze their fragrant essence shed;
And trees dispers'd, whose form their nature show,
Less prone to rise than branch in peace below:
So distant those, they seem, to fancy's eye,
To shun the spot that rears a fellow nigh;
Or, loathing crowds, had from the woods retir'd,
Or, proud of bulk, came forth to be admired.
A winding walk through this enchantment steals,
Where the deep dell a chaste abode reveals.
A shelving hill, of rock and heath, behind,
Conceals the dome and shields it from the wind;
A space before a holly hedge defends,
A tinkling gate communication lends,
Which past, the eye's enraptured with a view
Of fragrant flowers, adorn'd in every hue,

In mounds arranged with taste and neatly drest,
Which verdant bounds of well-shorn box invest;
Round these you're led by paths of golden dye
To where the low-built mansion meets the eye;
A neat thatch'd roof o'erspreads its whiten'd walls,
A vine's fond tendrils round its bosom crawls;
For light and air on either side is seen
A vitreous bow, which wears a face of green;
Distanced alike, a door the two divides,
With tutor'd woodbines climbing up its sides;
Uniting o'er, a flowery arch is made,
Which odour yields to all who seek its shade.
Its state internal no neglect betrays;
In modest neatness, taste the whole displays;
No want it feels, no luxury it shares,
Objects for use, but none for show it wears,
Save a few emblems on the mantel's height,
And a few landscapes which engage the sight,
And those, embellish'd with no common powers,
The sweet beguilings of an inmate's hours,
Who traced with fervor, or with fondness rear'd
Some child of fancy, or some scene endear'd.

The sober matron of the household store
The serious weight of threescore winters bore,

But, prone to action and by temperance fed,
Health's roseate bloom still o'er her features spread.
Cast on, in youth, that intermediate state
That lies between the lowly and the great,
To pass enabled life on either side,
As fate or chance her destiny might guide;
Assiduous bent, and flexible to bow,
Should fortune fall and mix her with the low;
Of sense possess'd, accomplishments and ease
That would, in scenes more elevated, please;
And,—what defects proud prejudice might find,
Bright gems enrich'd of every moral kind.

Full sixteen springs to this delightful glade
Her tuneful tribute Philomel had paid,
Since here she came in solitude to dwell,
But who, none knew, and none from whence could tell.
The curious sifted, others showed surprize,
And rumour spread what falsehood could surmise;
But truth and virtue from her dwelling stole,
And shed some ray still fatal to the whole;
Each baneful drop some beam of merit dried,
Conjecture sunk, and defamation died.

Mov'd in her train, and much her care engross'd,
A child, whose years four summers' suns had cross'd,
Whose opening gems, and charms of mental kind,
Which pleas'd the eye, and charm'd to love the mind,
Led fancy forward fondly to presume,
When one should ripen and the other bloom,
Of nature's gifts she would a store unfold,
Sweet to the sense and lovely to behold.

Attention watch'd, as comprehension grew,
And spread fresh stores of knowledge to her view,
And taught her fancy that its useful powers
Would soften nature and delight the hours,
And lead the mind by its enlightening beams
To that pure fount whence flow life's hopeful streams.

With life's best fruits was thus her reason charged,
Her mind delighted and her sense enlarged;
Truth o'er the treasure ruled with conscious sway,
And virtue awed each passion that would stray;
Mild temperance taught her where her confines went,
Nor farther prudence e'er her wishes sent.

And with the needy shar'd the comforts given,
And show'd the wealthy a sure way to Heaven.

So have I seen, where potent springs abound,
The water play in foaming eddies round,
But shun the tumult as its whirls subside,
And peaceful down its smooth-worn channel glide,
Where long its pure unsullied course it held,
By storm nor ruffled, nor by flood impell'd,
And gave to Nature solace as it went,
And to the world a placid mirror lent.

* * * * *

WRITTEN IN ALNWICK CASTLE,
November, 1823.

Oh! splendid old Alnwick, how glorious to trace
  In the lines which thy records contain,
The daring exploits which ennobled the race
  Of the Lords of thy ancient domain.
In the old feudal times, when the foe dared thy might,
  And thy vassals were zealous and brave,
Thy valorous chiefs, ever first in the fight,
  Or courted renown or a grave.

And many and bold were the bands that assail'd
  The peace of thy sumptuous halls;
And daring intruders, more distant, prevail'd,
  Which called for redress from thy walls;
But the rude hand of time hath now swept them away,
  And levell'd their domes to his will;
  Whilst thou art seen tow'ring more proudly to-day,
  And a Percy the lord of thee still.

But the mild rays of reason which beam on the earth,
   Have left those dark customs behind,
And man, who ferocity learnt from his birth,
   Is become in his nature refined;
Good fellowship reigns, and benevolence sheds
   Her solace in every degree,
And bright is the stream, and benignly it spreads,
   Of her fount which arises in thee.

The loud northern blast o'er thy turrets may blow,
   When winter thy portals invests,
Such excellence dwells in thy bosom below,
   Such welcome and cheer for thy guests,
That the season's unfelt, whilst the needy around,
   O'er whom thy indulgence prevails,
In the strains of eulogium mingle their sound,
   And send forth thy praise on the gales.

By the pillars of time may thy head be upheld,
   And ages yet pride in thy name,
As the emblems are traced of thy sons who excell'd
   In the proud emulations of fame.
May the currents of wealth which now flow in thy way,
   Ne'er cease in their ardour to run;
Nor the name, nor the race of thy chieftain decay,
   Till the last thread of time shall be spun.

THE WORLD'S LIKE A TYRANT, &c.

The world's like a tyrant and ruthless to me,
No solace it yields, and none beaming I see,
Tho' rugged my way, and I'm laden with care,
No rest can I find with the burthen I bear.

I have borne it till weary; yet time, as I go,
Progressively adds to my measure of woe;
Oh! would it were full, and more heavily prest,
And that to earth's bosom it sunk me to rest.

That my sleep will be sweet in the cradle of death,
And my spirit rejoice in the stillness of breath,
Is a comfort, by hope, thus in whisperings given,
' There! there! thou shalt rest,' and it pointeth to
    Heaven.

LAVER'S BANKS.

To woo the morning air
   On Laver's banks I stray'd,
And who should wander there
   But a lovely lonely maid.
Who stood and on the streamlet gazed,
   Till tears fell from her eye.
And mingled with the waters clear
   That slowly murmured by.

To learn her source of woe
   I asked in accents mild,
And if I could not comfort
   Afford to sorrow's child?
She said she wept for forms most dear,
   For ever from her gone,
And whom from early childhood
   She had lov'd to look upon.

Affection's tender eye
  A mother sought in vain,
They had laid her in the grave
  Where her father long had lain.
It touch'd the secret chord of love,
  And woke the heart to mourn,
When thinking, like the passing stream,
  They never would return.

I said, thou lovely maiden,
  Thy tears of sorrow stay;
The source still feeds the stream
  As the waters pass away;
And from the heavenly fount of life
  The current still flows on,
Affording blessings on its way
  For those for ever gone.

With those who sleep in death
  Be all thy cares resign'd,
And turn on life a cheerful eye,
  And thou shalt comfort find.
Oh! would'st thou crown a wish but now
  Become my bosom's guest,
I'd make thee mine and love thee dear,
  And lull thy cares to rest.

As leaves in autumn die
  Unsuccour'd on the spray,
Her woes uncherish'd in the mind
  Stole silently away.
And soon her tender heart grew charm'd
  In love's soft glowing beam,
And now we bless the happy morn
  We met by Laver's stream.

MY MARY IS NO MORE!

The airy choir the morning greets
  With harmony divine,
The verdant spring with flow'ry sweets
  Strews every path but mine.
My hopeful scenes of life are past,
  My dreams of bliss are o'er,
My love's sweet rose its bloom hath cast,
  My Mary is no more!

Her voice surpass'd in tuneful powers
  The sweetest birds that sing,
Her charms excell'd the fairest flowers
  That scent the breath of spring;
A soul more pure, a heart more kind,
  So fair a form ne'er bore,
And oh! what rays illumed her mind!
  But Mary is no more!

This blooming flower, so sweet and fair,
   On me its fragrance shed,
I gave it all my love and care,
   And hope my wishes fed;
But e'er I cull'd the lovely gem
   The spoiler stept before,
And pluck'd it rudely from its stem,
   And Mary is no more!

Celestial maid! she's call'd to share
   The sweetest joys of heaven;
Her form was deem'd a bliss too rare
   To mortal to be given.
Yet fancy still pourtrays her near,
   And views her o'er and o'er,
Whilst beaming in each eye, a tear
   Says, Mary is no more!

REFLECTIONS

ON VISITING A SPRING AT DIFFERENT SEASONS OF THE YEAR.

'Twas early in summer, and mild was the ray
Which beam'd from the sun on the waning of day;
And the air was serene, and the leaves on the trees
Were hardly emotion'd, so soft was the breeze;
The birds were in song in the wood on the hill,
And softly a murmur arose from the rill
Which ran thro' the mead, where its channel was seen,
By herbage more rude, and more tufted and green;
The teams, clinking home, had the fallow resign'd,
And whistling the ploughmen their cares to the wind,
When, pensive and slow, up the hamlet I bent,
And meeting the stream on its margin I went;
I stray'd to the spot whence it sprang from the earth,
Most pure in its nature and silent its birth;
It ran from a mound with green moss o'erspread,
Its birth-place was shaded by shrubs at its head;
'Twas onward impell'd by its kindred more strong,
And driven from home it went murmuring along.

In indolent ease on the bank I reclin'd,
And gazed on the stream, till awoke in my mind
A thought of the joys in its windings 'twould yield,
To the birds of the air and the beasts of the field,
To the web-footed tribe on its surface that ride,
And the bright-speckled trout in its bosom that glide,
To the poor thirsty beggar who drinks in his palms,
And softens the crusts he obtains for his alms;
To the thrifty old dame who, with low-bowing head,
Shall search it for cresses, to barter for bread;
To the youth who, in groups, on its borders shall
    play,
And launch their frail barks to be wreck'd in a day;
To the low in their need, and the high in their pride,
Who tenant the domes which are rear'd by its side,
And I mentally said, as in beauty it ran,
" Flow on thou bright stream, thou'rt a blessing to
    man."

A hill rose before, which a clump of beech crown'd,
Beguiling its steeps, to its summit I wound,
And saw the smoke rise thro' the trees on the plain,
From a mansion which stood in a stately domain,
And my mind running in a contemplative stream,
The worthy possessor it took for its theme.

By wisdom admir'd, and by virtue belov'd,
In the sphere of the great, like a magnet, he mov'd;
His honour was firm, and his friendship esteem'd,
Its warmth rose a charm where its influence beam'd;
With nature serene, and with manners refin'd,
He heighten'd the glory and joy of mankind.

A stream of benevolence flow'd from his soul,
And o'er its endowments had pity control,
For succour, in need, from his hand to have dealt,
No roof was too low, if there honesty dwelt;
And thus to the dwellings of want he was led,
And the naked he cloth'd, and the hungry he fed,
Instructed the young, and supported the old,
In summer thro' heat, and in winter thro' cold.

The midways of life, with a laudable zeal
He trode, and was hail'd a promoter of weal;
And many a soul would, in gratitude, tell,
In an intricate case he had counsell'd him well.
And o'er the expanse, as my vision I spread,
I thought of the joys which his bounty had shed,
And I said, tho' on earth few thy equals may be,
To the spring at the mound, there's a likeness in thee.

The summer was gone, and the autumn was past,
And winter's stern mandates were borne on the blast,

So ruthless it reign'd in its scourge of distress,
The sun lost its strength, and sweet nature her dress.
The birds in sad silence their grievances bore,
The red-breast alone sang for crumbs at my door;
All barren the plains, and the herds, by the cold,
Were chas'd from the pastures, and fed in the fold.
I listen'd, but heard not a sound from the stream,
My eye on the fallow discern'd not a team;
The ploughman's shrill notes, too, had ceas'd to be rife,
His hands begg'd his breath at the threshold of life.
To the streamlet, when wrapt in my mantle, I sped,
But its motion was still'd, and its visitants fled;
No float on its surface was gliding its way,
No object was seen on its bosom to play,
No draught it afforded, no charm it display'd,
Its beauty was lost when its bounty was staid;
Those souls, in whose need, 'twas not wont to deny,
Now wound from earth's bosom, by toil, a supply;
And yet, by its source, 'twas in amplitude fed,
But, chill'd at its birth, it lay useless and dead;
And I thought of the tribe, that its state would deplore,
And I said, what a change since I saw thee before.
The hill I surmounted, 'twas bleak on the brow,
And dreary the view it afforded me now,

Their late golden plumes, from the trees had been torn,
Nor a hawberry left for a bird on a thorn;
The dome, on the plain, I was wont to admire,
Now show'd by its smoke a reduction of fire,
For death, like the season, a change had wrought there,
Man's comforter gone, and a miser his heir—
So deep in whose nature was avarice grown,
Tho' large his possessions, no bounty was shown.
Distress o'er the hamlet soon mournfully spread,
The poor unemployed, and their children unfed;
The sick on their pallets in wretchedness pined,
Their solace was gone, and its sources confined;
The dome was in sorrow's dark heraldry drest,
Its cheer was expended, and mirth was suppress'd;
The stalls were all vacant, the timber had bow'd,
No herds rang'd the meadows, the pastures were plough'd;
The old neighing favourites that stray'd o'er the ground,
Were led to the kennels, and slain for the hounds.
The cellars were emptied, the servants discharged,
Expenditure lessen'd, and income enlarged,
And I said, in thy soul there's a semblance reveal'd,
To the spring at the mound now 'tis cold and congeal'd.

To the cold cell of death soon the miser was borne,
And great was his grief from his hoards to be torn:
'Twas thought he would pass from his objects of love
Unregretted below, and unwelcom'd above.
Howe'er his disposal, his God may arrange,
The mortals were few who rejoic'd at the change;
For the currents of wealth which he damm'd, in his haste,
A prodigal turn'd into riot and waste;
Down courses voluptuous it stream'd to the brink,
And dry was each space where the thirsty would drink;
For sensual pleasures 'twas destined to flow,
Lured virtue from peace, and then sank her in woe.

And when a strong winter was loosing its hold,
To see what the scene might to fancy unfold,
I thought, to the spring as I wandered once more,
A resemblance it now to the prodigal bore.
As the air lost its sting, and the water its chains,
In wanton confusion it ran o'er the plains;
As the mass at its head was expent by the sun,
Its virtues were lost in the courses it run;
Its heart yet unsoften'd, a passage denied
To all whom its bounty once amply supplied;
Down easy descents it was sportively led,
And o'er surfaces fair devastation it spread.

Yet time, I thought, soon would its wand'rings arrest,
And objects again with its uses be blest;
But the wasture of wealth, the world long might lament,
For reckless is Man till his substance be spent.

MARY ST. CLAIR.

How my heart yearns for thee, Mary St. Clair,
Fondly it turns to thee, Mary St. Clair;
    Tho' pangs of hopeless care,
    Thou doom'st my breast to bear,
Still thou art cherish'd there, Mary St. Clair!

Till my heart cease to glow, Mary St. Clair,
Till my blood cease to flow, Mary St. Clair,
    Thy lovely form shall be
    Dearest on earth to me,
Tho' no kind word from thee soothes my despair.

Should I despairing die, Mary St. Clair,
Life, love, without thee, I never can bear;
    Follow my mournful bier,
    Let fall a grateful tear
O'er him who lov'd thee dear Mary St. Clair!

ORRAN AND BERTHA.

"Come, Bertha, the Spring is its influence shedding,
 O'er hill and o'er dale the gay verdure is spreading,
 The leaves clothe the branches, the birds are all
  wedding,
  The world looks around us both lovely and rare;
 Since bountiful Nature's such beauties exposing,
 Let's stray o'er the hills ere the day shall be closing;
 The dews will be falling, the birds will be dozing,
  Come! haste, my love, haste!" said the youth to
   the fair.

Her nature inclin'd to her lover's inviting,
The beauties of Spring to her heart were delighting,
Love's purest emotions her thoughts were exciting
 To scenes most congenial, its pleasures to share.
With Nature and Love every sentiment warming,
With smiles sweet and tender, in dress most adorning,
She look'd like the Spring in the freshness of morning,
 When Orran in his link'd the arm of his fair.

The scenes which the Winter had robb'd of their treasure
Were shunn'd, like to man under Fortune's displeasure,
But in their new vestments were greeted with pleasure
  By every tun'd bird which enlivens the air;
Their clothing was sweet and the music transporting,
The flowers on the breeze were their fragrance exporting,
The doves were heard cooing—the lambs were seen sporting,
  All yielding delight to the youth and his fair.

Here, through a green tuft, the pale primrose was peeping;
There, round a wild shrub, the sweet woodbine was creeping;
Each scene, in advance, had some joy in its keeping
  Congenial to love and beguileful of care;
Thus, charm'd in their progress, still charm'd they proceeded;
Now Nature, now Love, in engaging succeeded,
No thought was left vacant for Time, who, unheeded,
  Stole by, and was closing day's scene on the pair.

They stray'd o'er the hills every feature admiring,
Till day, for the loss of the sun, was expiring;
The clouds look'd as tho' they were something con-
    spiring
  To check in their glory the fond loving pair.
The birds in succession their harmony slighted,
Tll nature grew dim and no longer delighted,
" A wild storm's approaching, we shall be benighted,
  Come, haste, my love, haste," said the youth to the
    fair.

Their steps they retraced with what speed they could
    master;
The storm was revengeful, and hurried on faster,
Soon darkness o'erspread them, oh! luckless disaster,
  What troubles some mortals are destin'd to bear!
The hollow blast blew, and the rain began streaming,
And foam'd down the hills whilst the lightning was
    beaming,
The thunder roll'd loud, and the fair one was scream-
    ing,
  " Take comfort, my love!" said the youth to the fair.

" Oh! where is there comfort? alas! do but say, love—
Nor comfort nor hope will be found but with day, love,
Shall not we be wandering the long night astray, love?
  Oh! tell me, my Orran, and ease my despair."

"Hush! no, my love, no, all our cares are dispelling,
I now hear the stream that flows near to thy dwelling,
From each growing source 'twill with anger be swelling,
Come, haste, that in safety we pass it, my fair."

But through the dark night they were long in exploring
Their way to the stream, which was traced by its roaring,
When, wild, down the hills the rough torrents came pouring;
'Twas swell'd—that to pass it few mortals would dare.
"Oh! stay, my lov'd Bertha, oh! stay, e'er you venture,
I'll ford the rude waters; perchance in the centre
Too deep 'twill be found for love's treasure to enter;
Oh! stay, my love, stay," said the youth to the fair.

He plunged in the stream with a fond lover's pleasure,
He stemm'd the rough torrent its deep bed to measure,
No space was propitious to bear o'er his treasure,
His strength was exhausting, his heart worn with care;

He still persever'd, still love's ardour expos'd him,
Rude objects, borne down with the current, oppos'd him;
He struggled, 'twas vain, the deep waters enclos'd him,
And down with the flood he was forced from his fair.

She heard the last effort with which he contended,
She heard the last cry which his bosom expended,
She lists—yet again,—but the conflict was ended,
   No effort, no voice, and no Orran was there.
Bereft and forlorn, with such woes to confound her,
The loud clashing elements beating around her,
The day dawned, when frantic the villagers found her,
   Crying "Orran, why stay you so long from your fair?"

When loud beats the storm, to her woes it awakes her,
And o'er them she'll ponder till reason forsakes her,
And, carelessly robed, from her home will betake her,
   And lonely and sad to the waters repair:
And gaze on the stream, and bewail her adorer,
And fondly beseech it her love to restore her,
And say to each object that fleeteth before her,
   "Oh! tell him to haste with love's speed to his fair."

THE CHILDREN'S DIRGE
AT THE INTERMENT OF A GOLD FISH.

Little fish, whose lovely dye
Nature gave to charm the eye,
Magnified in water clear,
Gliding in thy glassy sphere
To and fro, in gold attir'd,
Proud and pleased to be admired;
We have seen thee in thy day,
Beaming bright and frisking gay,
Deeming not that death so true
Soon might come and change thy hue,
And that eyes which felt delight
Soon would wish thee out of sight;
But 'tis done, and life's no more,
All thy pride and glitter's o'er;
All thy charms have felt decay,
Admiration steals away.
Thou'st but play'd a pageant part,
Won the eyes without the heart;
What alone the eyes revere,
Goes like thee without a tear.

Little fish, thy life was spent
Not as life for us is meant;
We, however fair, must be
More adorn'd internally;
Not applause to wish to gain
By a course so light and vain;
Not by specious means excite
Love that vanishes with sight;
Not to trifle time away;
We have mental dues to pay.
We must store within the mind
All that sense and worth can find;
'Twill create affection strong,
Rooting deep and lasting long;
'Twill adorn us when in breath,
'Twill exalt us after death.

Here thy long night's bed is made,
Deep beneath the verdant blade;
Thou therein must lie and rot,
Turn to earth and be forgot;
But in this, thou simple thing,
Honour treats thee like a king.
Get thee in and hide from view,
Little golden fish, adieu!

AN EXCUSE
TO
A YOUNG LADY,
FOR NOT WRITING SOME VERSES ON HER BIRTH-DAY.

You ask on the day
Of your birth for a lay,
And like other themes of the kind,
It must run in a strain
(For young ladies are vain)
Of praise, both of person and mind.

But I'll wait, if you please,
For my own love of ease,
Your merits as well to requite;
They'll be better pourtray'd
When, by time and your aid,
They are brought more conspicuous to life.

WRITTEN FOR

A YOUNG LADY

TO PRESENT TO HER PARENTS ON THE FIRST DAY OF THE
YEAR 1825.

The morn's awoke that one year more
Gives Time to number with his score,
And adds, for youth that would aspire,
A step to climb a little higher;
But bears, alas! with less of will,
On burthen'd age more heavy still.

Though mild hath been, in rule the past,
It oft to ire provoked the blast,
And rous'd old Ocean into strife,
Who prodigal hath been of life;
And in its lingering latest hours
Man bent, contracted by its powers;
The air it arm'd, congeal'd the plains,
And nature left embound in chains.
When not an odour scents the breeze,
When only ice-drops pearl the trees,

And not a bird is heard to sing,
And not an insect on the wing,
And not to run is heard a rill;
In bondage earth, and labour still;
When hoary meads no verdure yield,
And famish'd flocks forsake the field,
And nature in her wide controul
Hath not a charm to soothe the soul;—
When in the dearth of joys to please,
You slumber in domestic ease,
Oh! have an hour of gloom beguil'd,
And hear the wish that moves your child.

Oh! may the stranger, newly told,
To you congenial scenes unfold;
And may no season, in its reign,
A rugged, evil hour contain,
But all be calm and all be kind,
To please the eye and soothe the mind;
The spring, refreshing, soft, and rare,
The summer blooming, sweet, and fair,
And autumn, in its bounty great,
And winter in its mildest state,
And may, in neither, ruthless storms
Defeat the hopes which reason forms.

May I, in mental powers, disclose
In every change, such worth as those;
Enticed along to sense and thought,
With care, and fond affection, taught;
May I fair buds of promise show,
And shed endearments as I go;
And may the blossoms of the mind
Diffuse the fragrance of its kind,
Until, matured by time, it bears
The fruits that bless a parent's cares.

LINES

ON PARTING FROM MISS H.

WHEN TWO YEARS OLD.

Thou lovely, sweet engaging dear!
Thy artless prattling tongue to hear,
Thy ways to trace, thy smiles to view,
Thy dimpled cheeks of rosy hue,
Make every heart enraptur'd move
With admiration, and with love.

Can I, who've borne thee in my arms
So oft,—thou dawning bud of charms!
Can I each tender thought repel,
And take a listless, cold farewell?
No, no, sweet child! from thee to part,
Creates emotions in my heart,
Which ne'er will be by aught repress'd,
Till time one thought shall lull to rest;
A thought that this fond look may be
The last I e'er may have of thee.

Where'er my wandering steps may stray,
Howe'er my thoughts may fade away,
Most dear will one for thee remain,
Till I nor stray nor think again.

May thine and every mortal's friend
His care to thee, and love, extend,
And shield thee thro' this vale of life,
In every scene of woe and strife!

But if, for thy eternal weal,
Tis meet thou should'st of sorrow feel,
To calm desire, or change the will,
To call some wandering thoughts from ill,
To train them in the track allow'd,
To curb the vain and bend the proud;
May but to thee enough be given
To show how sweet's the path to Heaven!

THOU TELL'ST ME, MY LOVE, &c.

Thou tell'st me, my love with thy bloom will be
    fleeting,
Or cool, like the eve, when the sun wears away;
But in thy fair bosom such virtues are meeting,
As love will ensure when thy beauties decay.
Then grieve not, if time throws a shade o'er each
    feature;
No loss of thy charms shall my favour controul,
Nor toil to secure them, but leave them to nature,
I love thee for those far more dear to the soul.

The Ivy so green, yon old structure entwining,
Withstands the rude shock of each tempest that
    blows,
And seems to its object more proudly inclining,
As, year after year, fast to ruin it goes;
And so on in years will I solace and bless thee,
Tho' time may be ruthless and prey on thy charms;
As Ivy—the ruin, I'll fondly caress thee,
Until the last relic shall fall from my arms.

But ere from the branches the pile may be shaken,
Some hand to the root may a weapon apply,
And from its attraction averse to be taken,
'Twill cling on its bosom repining, and die.
And thus, if by Fate, life's career to be ending,
A bow should be bent, and the shaft should be mine,
Reluctant to leave thee, my fond arms extending
More firmly around thee, I'd wither on thine.

LOUISA TO JULIA,

WITH A BUNCH OF FLOWERS,

ON HER BIRTH-DAY IN NOVEMBER.

Tho' dreary the season, and gloomy the hour,
The day hath a charm, and revered it shall be,
One thought it awakens, most sweet in its power,
It gave, in its kindness, a sister to me.

Then Julia, this bouquet accept on the day,
And give me a smile of regard in exchange;
In us, as in Winter, these show not decay,
The sweets of affection no season shall change.

TO MARIA,

ON HER BIRTH-DAY.

The pensive soul, with joys imprest,
Will trace the source from which they flow;
The grateful heart will know no rest,
Till it its fond emotions show;
Man's mind—research, his fear and love
Are led by this to realms above.

Whate'er in nature charms his eyes,
Whate'er mild form his heart holds dear,
His health, the bliss his friend supplies,
His night's repose, his daily cheer,—
Howe'er, on earth, to him they're given,
They flow from the pure fount of Heaven.

Yon tree, now waving in the wind,
Comes yearly bending with its fruit,
Shall it awake remembrance kind,
And not the power which gave it root?
Love wanting thought's too weak to rise,
Reflection bears it to the skies.

Now in the soft'nings of my care,
I feel, my friend, I'm largely bless'd,
By those sweet fruits of virtues rare
By Heaven implanted in thy breast;
Their bed my tenderest care shall be,
And He my praise who made it thee.

Yes! thou shalt be, beneath mine eye,
With friendship's mildest nurture fed,
And no vile weed shall come thee nigh,
And no rude foot shall on thee tread,
Nor in each season's keenest hour
Shall e'er my will repress my power.

May He, who with those fruits and flowers
Thy mind enrich'd, and graced thy form,
Refresh thee with congenial showers,
And shield thee from each ruthless storm!
That long each rising fair may find
A form by which to shape her mind.

TO A FRIEND OF EARLY LIFE,

ON HER BIRTH-DAY.

Does not the man of soul sincere,
Who holds his country's welfare dear,
Rejoice when noble deeds are done,
And battles fought, and victories won,
When Justice makes Oppression yield,
And Honour triumphs in the field?

Does not within his bosom bound
His heart, when time, revolving round,
A day unfolds, on which the Sun
Of Glory o'er his country shone,
And when his sires, with dauntless zeal,
Preferr'd to life, its fame and weal?

And such a soul shall comprehend
As sweet sensations for a friend,
Who, in domestic life, is great
As any pillar to the state;
Who treads the mazy scenes of youth
With honour, chastity, and truth;

Whose gentle heart's by nature kind,
Whose moral precepts charm the mind,
Who shuns the baneful haunts of strife,
And woos the tranquil scenes of life,
In whose whole course a charm's unfurl'd,
Which binds our natures to the world.

Now passing on from youth to age,
Where cares oppress in every stage,
Where lurking ills poor life annoy,
And aim a shaft at every joy;
Mild, from thy way, those virtues beam,
Illume my paths, and wake my theme;
Nor could I, conscious of thy worth,
Deny the day which gave thee birth,
To let my muse my thoughts rehearse,
In humble, but in grateful verse.

We, from the strange promiscuous throng,
Which crowd life's devious course along,
Were by our guide design'd to steer
Our way awhile, unsever'd here;
And many a rugged day, and rude,
When ills would frown, and cares obtrude,
We social aid each other lent,
To chase the gloom of discontent.

May long, my friend, our progress be
Through scenes remote from enmity;
But ne'er, to man, will fate disclose,
Or how it lies, or where it goes;
But tho' bedimm'd we thus advance,
Thro' turnings various, left to chance,
We still may trace where prudence sped,
And on with hope and cheerful tread;
Nor go shall prudence, cautious fair,
Through scenes that know no troubles there,
But those, my friend, tho' keenly felt,
Are Heaven's decrees, and kindly dealt.

Or if, from hence, our progress leads
Through dreary ways or flow'ry meads,
Or vales of bliss, or hills of care,
Or barren heaths of shelter bare,
How soon we each our road may change,
For fate will worldly schemes derange,
Our journey long, or period near,
He only knows who sent us here.

And He, alone, possesses power,
To shorten or prolong the hour;
He kens where tends man's restless will,
Unerring Judge of good and ill;

O'er weal and woe, control He wields,
And to the soul its portion deals;
Then should not man due reverence show
To Him, from whom his blessings flow,
By yielding thanks for those in store,
And humbly hoping still for more.

When, mingling on in life's advance,
Thou'lt meet at some strange turn of chance,
A soul of whom fate may approve
To lead thee down the paths of love,
Win sweet consent, become allied,
And bear thee hence a hopeful bride:
Whate'er new paths thy feet shall press,
Whate'er new friends thy form shall bless,
Whate'er new charms to thee reveal,
Oft o'er the past thy thoughts will steal;
And as on youthful scenes they dwell,
Of souls endear'd will memory tell,
When thus thy pensive mind shall stray,
And at this period pause and say,
In calms, in storms, in suns, and showers,
Here friendship cheer'd the passing hours.

LINES

WRITTEN FOR
MISS L. S. BRUERE TO PRESENT TO HER MOTHER
ON HER BIRTH-DAY.

Yon orb, my Mamma, the luminary of earth,
Beams bright on the morn of the day of my birth,
And fondly I come, ere it fades to the view,
To tender my heart's young emotions to you;
Emotions, Mamma, which instinctively rise,
With each thought of the form that gave light to mine eyes.

I bring, my Mamma, for affection and care,
As much as a bosom so tender can bear;
And am rearing a hope, that, as reason appears,
My love and my duty will strengthen with years;
And am nursing a thought, that, with you for my guide,
To solace your love, I may merit your pride.

To render, Mamma, as life's summit I gain,
Each step, as I rise, uncreative of pain,—
I'll aim, in advancing, with diligence kind,
To shape by your precepts the frame of my mind;
And its form will be pure, and its nature be mild,
Should your image, Mamma, be discern'd in your child.

LINES

ADDRESSED TO THE
MISSES L. AND T. SADLIER BRUERE,
ON THE FIRST DAY OF THE YEAR 1824.

Time's last son on record, the year that is dead,
Which left you in charge of the one in its stead,
In safety hath borne you, on land and by sea,
In sickness and sorrow, and left you in glee:
And may its successor, as well as the past,
In safety enshroud you in every rude blast!
For in worth, and in charms, ye are early and rife,
Two sweet little flowers in the garden of life,
As fresh as the rose, and as fair as the day,
And as mild and as sweet as the mornings in May.
Tho' tender in stalk, ye are lovely in hue,
Few flowers in the gardens more hopeful to view,
And long may ye bloom, and give joy to the eye,
Refresh'd by the dews which are shed from on high;
And still may the sense by your fragrance be charm'd,
As still by the rays of affection you're warm'd;
Expanding in thought, as you're cultur'd with care,
Till time shall have form'd you as perfect as fair!

May venomous weeds ne'er anigh you be found,
To poison your sweets, or unhallow the ground.
But still in the garden, two favourites, stay,
Till leaf after leaf of your bloom falls away;
And hence when remov'd, for the loss they sustain,
They who mourn you be bless'd with a hope of your gain,
A hope that, tho' lost to the world and its love,
To flourish more fair you're transplanted above!

LINES

WRITTEN FOR
MISS L. S. B. TO PRESENT TO HER MOTHER,
ON HER BIRTH-DAY,
WITH SOME PRIMROSES AND VIOLETS.

With primroses pale, and with violets blue,
The Spring hath the first robe of nature array'd,
I cull'd these with care, and I bring them to you,
From a sense that your love should with sweets be repaid.

They well will denote, to your vigilant eye,
The expansion of scenes more endear'd to the sight,
As the great orb of day shall ascend in the sky,
Sweet Nature will beam in her glory more bright.

On earth introduced with those sweetest of flowers,
May I, as with joy they the senses renew,
Inhaling their fragrance, inherit their powers,
And shed, in each season, a sweetness on you!

And if the advancement of charms they disclose,
In which the endowments of Nature combine,
May the sweets that I breathe have the virtue of those,
And gladden your heart with the progress of mine!

WRITTEN FOR A. S. B.

ON HIS BIRTH-DAY, WHEN EIGHT YEARS OLD,

DECEMBER 17th, 1828.

Yes! I'm advanced another year,
    Another's sunk behind me;
But who, when this shall disappear,
    Knows where the next may find me?
For, as the sun one day beams clear,
    And may the next be clouded,
I may to-day in life appear,
    And be to-morrow shrouded.

Since life is but a dubious state,
    And over its existence
Presides a Being good as great,
    I'll ask His kind assistance.
In climbing on from youth to age,
    And every year I heighten,
Let such pursuits my mind engage,
    As may in honour brighten.

Contending with my tasks of life,
  Some mazes may perplex me,
Which should be met with noble strife,
  Not irritate, nor vex me.
Such combats will exalt the soul,
  As still my journey lengthens,
And give the mind still more controul,
  As year by year it strengthens.

Sweet love and care were, day by day,
  Throughout the last, my portion,
And shall it from me pass away
  Without one fond emotion?
Oh no! a thought's most kindly felt
  For all the joys I'm knowing,
I love those souls by whom they're dealt,
  And Him from whom they're flowing.

May still such hopes beam from my mind
  As stimulate affection,
And still my guardian Angel find
  Me worthy of protection!
If, cheer'd by love and led by care,
  I gain life's highest station,
Oh, may my grateful spirit there
  Promote its own salvation!

ON THE DEATH OF LORD BYRON.

Thy destiny's cast and before thee;
   And sever'd thy body and breath,
Thou'rt left, and the Muses deplore thee,
   On the dark and cold desert of death.

The strains of thy lyre were enchanting,
   And bore over nature controul,
But yet was another chord wanting,
   To attune it more sweet to the soul.

The sound that's to merit inspiring,
   Its sweet introduction to love,
And cheering to worth in aspiring
   To a seat with the blissful above.

Tho' reckless of these was thy story,
   And left to more impotent lays,
The Corsair shall glow in thy glory,
   The Wanton shall bask in thy praise.

The isle of thy birth is the rarest,
   Thy home was the proudest to have,
The fair of her soil are the fairest,
   The bravest, her sons, of the brave.

The land of thy sires was forsaken,
   Its worthies thy genius abused,
No pride in her virgins was taken,
   Its sons were a tribute refused.

In climes now inglorious a ranger,
   With passions unbridled and strong,
Love's current was turn'd on the stranger,
   And the dissolute nurs'd in thy song.

Had thy fame and thy country's together
   In an orbit conjunctively shone,
'Twould have beam'd on illuming each other,
   Till Time had extinguish'd the sun.

ON THE BATTLE OF WATERLOO.

In storm and tempest arose the day,
   Which show'd the foe to view,
Who, vain and impatient for the fray,
   Aloud the onset blew;
     And the fight with vengeful ire began,
     And the fire in ceaseless thunder ran,
     From line to line, and from man to man,
   Death's shafts destructive flew.

The hearts were brave, and the bands were strong,
   Which hope led to the field,
The fight was fierce, and the strife was long,
   And neither host would yield:
     When many valorous deeds were done,
     And the day by patient prowess won,
     Then on England's triumph set the sun,
   And the foe could find no shield.

And those who oft for glory fought,
    Were doomed no more to know,
But now, in their speed their safety sought,
    And death kept with the slow;
        For a band unwearied in the fight,
        By wrongs provoked, pursued their flight,
        And many lay, ere the morning's light,
    Down on their gorgets low,

Now pity o'er the brave prevail'd,
    Who trod the field of gore,
And many a bold heart's mansion hail'd,
    To ask if life was o'er:
        'Twas long from some choice spirits fled,
        And the last chill'd drop some just had bled,
        But many maim'd from among the dead,
    And off the field, they bore.

And many sigh'd for a comrade lost,
    Who had cheer'd his arduous hours;
And many a weeping fair was cross'd,
    By love's disastrous powers;
        And yet there beam'd through their grief a pride,
        For the envious deaths their heroes died,
        Which might have been thro' tears descried,
    Just like the sun in showers.

And the scene shall long fond thoughts renew,
   Tho' tears bedim the eye;
And long, with that field of fame in view,
   Shall a Briton's heart beat high,
     Who treads the soil where the valiant fell,
     And views the mounds which their ashes swell,
     And reads the tombs which their glories tell,
In Belgium where they lie.

POOR KITTY.

No joy in early youth denied,
    No thought adverse distress'd me;
My parent's care my wants supplied,
    Who to their bosoms press'd me;
But death, whose power no arm can brave,
    Or plaints arrest of pity,
Hath borne them from me to the grave,
    And friendless left poor Kitty.

No home wherein to hide my head,
    No earthly friend to guide me,
Too young in years to earn my bread,
    Whatever will betide me!
A wandering, houseless child of care,
    A candidate for pity,
If bless'd by Heaven with aught to spare,
    Relieve the wants of Kitty!

By early admonitions taught
  That life's beset with danger,
It fills with dread, and pains with thought,
  An unprotected stranger.
If shelter'd from its snares awhile,
  Beneath some roof of pity,
What fervent prayers with Heaven's smile
  Would bless the friends of Kitty!

LINES

OCCASIONED BY READING THE FOLLOWING PRINTED BILL, FIXED IN THE BEAK OF ONE IN A GROUP OF FIVE STUFFED OWLS IN THE SHOP WINDOW OF A BIRD STUFFER, AT RICHMOND, YORKSHIRE.

"We five owls were once alive;
On birds and mice we used to thrive;
Through barns and towers oft did fly
In search of prey both wet and dry,
And on each shining summer's day
In hollow trees we pass'd our time away,
Till the cruel sportsman forc'd us to the field,
Then unto the gun we were obliged to yield;
But now we have undergone dissection,
To add and join this grand collection.
Glass eyes we have got and cannot see,
Spectacles are of use, but not to we;
Now no more birds or mice we pursue,
For we are stuff'd, and it is true,
By Mr. Stevenson,—who stuff'd us five,
And hundreds more, as though they were alive.

W. STEVENSON,
Stuffer of Birds, Animals, Reptiles, and Fish;
Dealer in Fishing-Tackle,
Richmond, Yorkshire."

Indeed, ye five,
Were ye alive?
Was wisdom doom'd to suffer?
And did your brains
Reward the pains
Of Stevenson your stuffer?

Why in his lines
Such merit shines,
The wonder now is known;
He, vain pretence,
Purloin'd your sense,
And pass'd it for his own!

The fraud forgive;
Your fame will live,
And pass to future times,
And long the sight
And sense delight,
In feathers and and in rhymes.

May, to the six,
From chance and tricks,
Be kind protection given!
The owls are worth
The charge of earth;
The man, the care of Heaven!

ON THE DEATH OF GAFFER GUN.

Poor old Gaffer Gun,
Thy labour is done,
The sod thou shalt sever no more;
Thy doublet and flail
Are hung on a nail,
But the corn's left undress'd on the floor.

The Lord of the soil
Set a time for thy toil,
Tho' thy work should be left in the rough;
And true to the hour,
Invested with power,
Death came, and cried " Gaffer, enough!"

With insight profound,
As the season came round,
To thy sickle and scythe thou'dst an eye;
But ere the corn's brown
Thou, alas! art cut down,
And now in death's stack-yard must lie.

And when to be tried,
Soul and body divide,
May thy sins be, as chaff, lightly driven;
But as grain, bright and sound,
May thy spirit be found,
And 'twill meet a good market in Heaven.

TO A GENTLEMAN

WHO MARRIED A SECOND WIFE THREE DAYS AFTER THE INTERMENT OF HIS FIRST.

Says the moral divine,
" 'Tis a sin to repine
At whatever fate may ordain thee;
Be it mild or severe,
'Tis the best for thee here,
From sorrow 'tis wise to refrain thee."

And wisdom thou'st shown,
In a loss of thine own,
A form once ador'd beyond measure;
Thy grief lost its hold,
As the object grew cold,
And thy heart soon was wean'd of its treasure.

And Heaven was kind
To a soul so resign'd,
And favour'd thee more than another;
As Death thro' one door
A faded joy bore,
Love danced with one in at the other.

And give it thy care!
For many's the fair
More slow would have been to endear thee;
But, panting for breath,
And undaunted by death,
She ran to caress and to cheer thee.

Slow wooers impart,
That the springs of the heart
Take patience and time in discerning,
But, quick-sighted dears,
You saw, thro' your tears,
Love's passion was mutually burning.

But, 'twas reckless to pay,
By three days delay,
The useless expense of a carriage;
In that which you rode
To death's dark abode,
You might have return'd from your marriage.

And what tongues would have told,
How you went with a cold—
But soon you return'd with a warm one;
And fame would have ran
With the worth of the man
Possessed of such powers to charm one.

MY NOSE.

What leads me on where'er I go,
In sun and shade, in joy and woe,
Thro' fog and tempest, rain and snow?
      My Nose.

In youth's most ardent reckless day,
And when arose disputes at play,
What would be foremost in the fray?
      My Nose.

And should my tongue rude blows provoke,
What would protrude and brave each stroke,
Till coral streams its pains bespoke?
      My Nose.

And falling in an airy bound,
In chase of some new charm or sound,
To save me—what came first to ground?
      My Nose.

When some dark pass I would explore,
With neither shut nor open door,
What oft for me hard usage bore?
My Nose.

And when in want I yearn'd to eat,
And hunger might my judgement cheat,
What prompted me to food most sweet?
My Nose.

Mid violet banks and woodbine bowers,
And beds where bloom'd the fairest flowers,
What fed me with their fragrant powers?
My Nose.

Each eye may need in age a guide,
And when young helpmates I provide,
Thy back thou'lt lend for them to stride,
My Nose.

And can I or in care or glee,
Refuse my aid and love to thee,
Who thus hast felt and bled for me,
My Nose?

No; when cold winter's winds blow high,
And bite thee hard, and thou shalt cry,
Thy tears with sympathy I'll dry,
      My Nose.

And if for snuff thy love shall come,
Thy slaves, my finger and my thumb,
Shall faithful be, and bear thee some,
      My Nose.

Still as I follow thee along,
Oh! may'st thou never lead me wrong,
But thou must hush our sleeping song,
      My Nose!

FROM A COBLER TO B.

ON RETURNING HIM AN OLD PAIR OF SHOES.

Your shoes have I look'd o'er and o'er,
   And tell you as a friend,
The more I look'd, I thought the more
   Their case too bad to mend.

Their seams are rent, and soles abused,
   Beyond my art's redress;
Their upper parts, more rudely used,
   Seem weeping in distress.

Had they not turn'd aside, I ween,
   Thro' your untoward ways,
They might their maker's pride have been,
   And borne you many days.

But keep then steadfast in your mind;
   Expose them on a shelf,
And well they'll serve you to remind
   A sinner of himself.

Oh! think, like these may be your plight,
    As you their state discern,
Should you not mend and walk upright,
    Ere you too old are worn.

And should you mend, and Man shall cry,
    What brought vice to a close?
Raise to the shelf a reverend eye,
    And say, " 'Twas those old shoes."

And with your name bequeath them down,
    And earnestly desire,
That every rising race be shown,
    What turn'd from sin its sire.

VERSES

WRITTEN FOR A BOY TO LEARN AND REPEAT WHO HAD COMMITTED A SMALL THEFT.

Oh God! whose searching eye doth see
    Mine every deed— ill done or well—
No thought of mine's unknown to thee;
    Unknown is no untruth I tell.

A liar's tongue dost thou disclaim,
    Against a thief denouncest woe;
And all who vilify thy name
    Are punish'd in the gulf below.

An act of theft my name hath stain'd,
    Which I denied with daring vow;
But injur'd truth my guilt proclaim'd,
    And conscious shame o'erwhelms me now.

How much, O God, my crime offends,
    How ruthful its effect appears;
Displeas'd art Thou, and mortal friends;
    And dim a father's eyes with tears.

But with that kind, benignant aid,
   Which Thou canst give and I implore,
I'll seek the path from which I stray'd,
   And swerve from them and Thee no more.

But hope, and aim, in life to be
   What truth and virtue may approve;
And glorify and honour Thee,
   And recompense a parent's love.

A PRAYER IN AFFLICTION.

Thou Maker of all things, Thou Lord of all living,
   Thou whom to thy creatures such wonders disclose,
Oh! look down with mercy benign and forgiving,
   And chase from my turbulent bosom its woes.

Or grant, if affliction shall still be thy pleasure,
   That ne'er, to evade it, I wander astray;
But make of those precepts my soul's dearest treasure,
   Thou hast set forth to guide us on life's troubled way,

Then, tho' in my progress rude storms may assail me,
   And in a world selfish no shelter be given,
As darkness enclose me, I'll hope Thou wilt hail me,
   And bid me repose in the mansion of heaven.

AN EPITAPH

ON

PHILIP AND MARY JONES.

Grim Death conceals beneath these stones,
The mortal part of Philip Jones,
Where erst his wife, poor Sarah, lay,
And fast they now return to clay.

Tho' life exalts thine head on high,
Look pensive down on where they lie;
And know, howe'er with gifts endow'd,
How rich or poor, how meek or proud,
Time levels all to one degree,
And soon what they are thou shalt be.

Be just, like them, that death may deal
The latest pang thou'rt doom'd to feel;
That when to earth thy body's given,
Thy soul may find repose in Heaven.

LINES

ON

THE DEATH OF MISS SADLIER BRUERE,

WHO DIED, AND WAS INTERRED BY THE SIDE OF MISS BURNET, WHO WAS BURIED BUT A FEW DAYS BEFORE HER, AT BRIGHTON, SEPTEMBER, 1828, AGED 22.

Tours, December 1, 1828.

Thou wert seen, faded blossom with joy and endear'd
As the first of thy kind on the stem that appear'd;
Thou wert watch'd with affection, and hope with thee grew,
As, with promise, thy form still expanded to view;
Thou wert come to the period when nature displays
The sweets with which time for her culture repays,
And when to the world thou wert opening in bloom,
Thou wert chill'd by the blast, and enclos'd in a tomb.

Thou wert miss'd in the group when the eye look'd around,
And miss'd by the ear was thy voice in the sound,
Thy chamber was darksome, thy bell was unrung,
Thy footstep unheard, and thy lyre unstrung:

A stillness prevail'd at the mournful repast;
In tears was the eye on thy vacant seat cast;
Each scene wearing gloom, and each brow bearing care,
Too plainly denoted that death had been there.

Thou wert laid by the side of thine emblem in years;
Ere dry was her grave thine was moisten'd with tears:
And ye hold to the world a joint lesson of truth,
That life is not safe in the keeping of youth.
Could care avert death, and the heart's treasure save,
Ye had not been doom'd to a premature grave,
Now ye sleep on the hill by the sea-beaten shore,
And the voice of the storm shall awake ye no more.

To earth we consign'd thee, and made an advance,
The thought to beguile, to the vineyards of France.
But 'twould not be cheated; of all that was rare,
Fond nature kept whispering a wish thou could'st share:
No air softly swelling, no chord struck with glee,
But awoke in the bosom remembrance of thee.
Even now, as the cold winds adown the leaves bring,
We sigh that our flow'ret was blighted in spring.

Life's pilgrimage is but a trial of trust,
And bliss, at its period, the meed of the just.
Why then should we mourn thee, with sigh or with tear,
And at thy advancement in trouble appear?
To the home which thou'rt gone to we're destin'd to go,
And the further we journey the greater our woe.
To thee, more deserving, the favour was given,
To pass, whilst we wander, a near road to Heaven.

TO

OUR WORTHY SHEPHERD, MR. WAY,

ON HEARING OF HIS REARING SOME YOUNG WOLVES.

Tours, June, 1829.

———

As the sheep of the fold
Whom your Rev'rence has told
   The sinful and vile to be loathing,
And of wolves to beware,
For, without moral care,
   They'll steal on the flock in sheep's clothing;

We, alas! Mr. Way,
Must distrust what you say,
   When next you entreat us to heed them;
When, leaving us then,
You go home to their den
   With fatherly fondness to feed them.

May our Shepherd above
Keep us still in your love,
    Though the wolves may a portion inherit;
If those must prevail
O'er the flesh, which is frail,
    Let us be illumed with the Spirit.

LONDON:
PRINTED BY C. ROWORTH, BELL YARD,
TEMPLE BAR.